Books by Rene Noorbergen:

The Death Cry of an Eagle
Nostradamus—Invitation to a Holocaust
Secrets of the Lost Races
The Soul Hustlers
Programmed to Live
The Ark File
Charisma of the Spirit
Ellen G. White—Prophet of Destiny
You Are Psychic
Jeane Dixon—My Life and Prophecies

The DEATH CRY of an EAGLE

*The Rise and Fall of Christian Values
in the United States*

*Rene Noorbergen
and Ralph W. Hood*

**ZONDERVAN
PUBLISHING HOUSE** OF THE ZONDERVAN CORPORATION
GRAND RAPIDS, MICHIGAN 49506

To Arthur and Gladys Damon,
two Plymouth octogenarians,
and to Laura and Linda.

Rene Noorbergen
Ralph W. Hood

Illustrations by Martha Bentley

THE DEATH CRY OF AN EAGLE
Copyright © 1980 by Rene Noorbergen and Ralph Hood

Library of Congress Cataloging in Publication Data

Noorbergen, Rene.
   The death cry of an eagle.

   1. United States—Moral conditions. 2. Christianity and culture. I. Hood, Ralph
W., joint author. II. Title.
HN90.M6N66   973   80-25125
ISBN 0-310-30431-8

Unless otherwise indicated, all Scripture quotations are from *The Holy Bible: The New
International Version,* copyright © 1978 by the New York International Bible Society.
Used by permission.

Printed in the United States of America

Contents

Chapter One
  In the Beginning 9

Chapter Two
  An Anxious Nation 31

Chapter Three
  God Moves in History 54

Chapter Four
  Destruction of a Golden Empire 69

Chapter Five
  The Failure of Reason 81

Chapter Six
  The Grandeur That Was Rome 93

Chapter Seven
  Is There a Formula for Decline? 113

Chapter Eight
  The Death Cry of an Eagle 131

Chapter Nine
  The Missing Soul of the Nation 163

Chapter Ten
  Where Does America Go From Here? 178

Notes 187

The DEATH CRY of an EAGLE

Chapter One

In the Beginning

There is a beginning to everything—even to national greatness. We were reminded of this a short time ago when we stood silently in a small dusty room and let our eyes wander fondly over a yellowing page in *Journal G. fol. 33*, one of the many volumes in the aging city archives of the Dutch city of Leiden.

The wording was simple, yet impressive:

Request by 100 persons, born in England, to be allowed to take up residence in this town.

To the Honourable the Burgomaster and the Court of the City of Leyden.

With due respect and submissiveness, JAN ROBARTSEN, Minister of God's Holy Word, together with some hundred people, born in the Kingdom of Great Britain, to the number of some hundred people or thereabouts, men as well as women, let you know that they should like shortly to come and settle in this town, that is by May next, and to get the freedom of the town to earn their living with various of their trades without being a burden to anyone. Therefore the petitioners apply to your Honour earnestly praying that your Honours would grant them free and liberal consent to betake themselves as aforesaid.

And your petitioners will ever pray.

(*signed*) John Robinson

In the margin of this desperate request was this resolution:

The Court, making a disposition of the present request, declare that they do not refuse honest persons free and liberal entrance into this town, and to settle there, provided they will behave themselves honourably, and submit to all laws, and regulations of this town, and that therefore the coming of the petitioners will be welcome to them.

Thus done in their session at the townhall, this twelfth of February, 1609.

(*signed*) J. van Hout

For the "Pilgrims" it was the beginning of a new phase in their persevering search for freedom.

For a number of years considerable tension had been building up between the English Christians who had chosen to adhere to the purity and simplicity of the primitive church on one side, and the ever-growing political ambitions of the government-supported English church on the other. Finally religious liberty was curtailed to such an extent that it caused great moral conflict. When church attendance became required by law under penalty of imprisonment, deportation, or death, it became obvious to the Separatists that there was only one way out—voluntary exile. The nineteenth-century writer E. G. White comments,

Hunted, persecuted and imprisoned, they could discern in the future no promise of better days, and many yielded to the conviction that for such as would serve God according to the dictates of their conscience, "England was ceasing forever to be a habitable place."

Some at last determined to seek refuge in Holland. Difficulties, losses and imprisonment were encountered. Their purposes were thwarted, and they were betrayed into the hands of their enemies. But steadfast perseverance finally conquered, and they found shelter on the friendly shores of the Dutch Republic.[1]

The request for political asylum as recorded in the city archives was made about the time that William Brewster named his third child Fear, as a reminder of the continuous torment suffered by him and other separatist "Brownists." The persecution became so severe that removal to Holland seemed to be the only alternative. This idea is not surprising, since the "Republic of the United Netherlands" had just surfaced from a bloody war with Spain over religious freedom. So widespread was the European admiration of Dutch liberality and toleration that the tiny country was often referred to as "the great ark of the refugees" and "Amsterdam, the fair of all the sects, where all the pedlars of religion have leave to vend their toys."[2]

From this humble nucleus of religious refugees seeking a safehold in the Netherlands came the voyage of the *Speedwell* and the *Mayflower*—and eventually the growth of the American republic.

But although we are all familiar with the basics of that story, do we really know the background?

The same archives that have so carefully preserved the original Pilgrims' request for refuge also contain documents relating the position of the host government when the British crown complained bitterly about the Dutch giving sanctuary to a group of British outcasts.

The Leiden city fathers responded:

> In reply to it we hold that the Honourable Wynwod, ambassador of His Majesty the King of Great Britain, is wrongly informed that we should have entered into a composition with some of the Brownists.

It is true that in February last we got a request from Jan Robarts, minister of the Divine Word, together with some of the Christian reformed religion, born in England, in which they asked for permission to take up their abode in the town of Leyden. Thereupon we have resolved and declared that we did not refuse honest people free and liberal entrance, provided that they should behave honourably and submit to the laws and regulations of this town, and that the petitioner should be welcome as may be seen from the request and the accompanying resolution of which your Honour will find copy enclosed, without anything else having been done by us.

We have never known and do not know now that the petitioners should have been exiled from England and that they should belong to the Brownist Sect.

This document is not dated, but judging from the organization of the archives, it is clear that it dates prior to April 30, 1609.

That Great Britain was greatly displeased with the United Netherlands' hospitality toward the group was obvious from the start, yet there was a short period of courteous hesitation before the British crown attempted to interfere. Following their escape from England, the group first settled in Amsterdam, but a search of that city's archives has not yielded a protest similar to the one regarding Leiden.

The new arrivals were only part of the constant influx of refugees who crowded the streets of old Amsterdam. Assorted aristocrats such as Frederick V, Elector Palatine, King of Bohemia; the queen of Charles I, Henrietta Maria; and many groups—namely the Separatists, Brownists, Baptists, Fifth Monarchy Men, Huguenots, Walloons, had already paved the way. The Pilgrims—unsophisticated as they were—wandered wide-eyed through the bustling streets of the city and were barely noticed. For a short interval they settled in Bruinistengang with John Smythe's Ancient Brethren, but because of their inability to tolerate the religious beliefs of the other Separatists, John Robinson and William Brewster ultimately realized that a parting was inevitable, and they moved twenty-five miles away to

Leiden, "a city fair and beautiful and of a sweete situation." After knocking at the city gates, John Robinson submitted his petition for group citizenship.

A growing measure of religious intolerance that surfaced among the freedom-loving group was not the only reason for leaving Amsterdam. The countryside was beautiful, yet the commercial center had its shortcomings. Sir William Brereton wrote in his book *Travels* that Amsterdam was

> a most flourishing city yet the air so corrupt and unwholesome especially in winter time, when most part of the country round about overflowed. Here no fresh water, no water to brew but what is fetched from six English miles distant. Hence they have much beer but no water to wash withal but rain water, little fire except turf the most of the wood burnt here brought out of Denmark and Norway. . . . The coals come from Newcastle.[3]

Obviously difficult as compared with existing conditions in Europe today, yet not at all uncommon in the Europe of the seventeenth century.

Leiden's standard of living could not have differed much from that of Amsterdam, but the many religious disagreements with the Ancient Brethren compelled John Robinson's group to leave. Skirting the Haarlemmermeer (an inland lake), they entered Leiden, anxious to rebuild their shattered lives.

Originally called "Leithen," it was already an important set-tlement about A.D. 800, some 90 years before the discovery of America and 809 years before the Pilgrims stood before the city gates asking for asylum. Known as the birthplace of Rembrandt van Rijn, Leiden, with the Rhine River running through its heart, opened its doors to the weary travelers.

Following the stipulation that "they will behave themselves honourably," they seriously tried to build up an English-style existence among the seafaring Dutch. But the "sweete situation" gradually evaporated as, according to Cotton Mather, the "grimme and grisly face of povertie came upon them like an armed man."[4] Huddled together in the slum environment of the

Stinksteeg (Stinkalley), the Separatists—husbandrymen all their lives—improvised as clumsy blacksmiths, hatters, tailors, weavers, glovers, and silk workers. Bradford himself joined the rapidly expanding weaving industry and became a maker of fustian—a coarse cotton cloth—while John Robinson engaged in ribbon making and teaching English to students at Leiden University, a most prestigious seat of learning in that part of Europe. Robinson eventually accumulated enough money to purchase a large house, the Green Gate, and built a small conclave of twenty-one tenements in the garden to shelter the other families. Robinson's new abode was near the university, where he spent much of his time in religious debate.

But it was in an entirely different field that William Brewster made a name for himself: printing. Whereas in his early years at Oxford he had been a leftist student and for a time enjoyed a diplomatic career "tainted" with the bawdy life of Shakespearean London, the continuing association with the intensely religious escapees greatly enriched his life. Splinter groups like the Separatists were always seeking means to disseminate the gospel they preached, and in this case, the press operated by Brewster, Edward Winslow, and Thomas Brewer became the production center for religious literature. Working underground, the three men managed to produce as many as twenty incendiary books, shipping them through Scotland into England in false-bottomed wine barrels. These small yet powerful sticks of literary dynamite so infuriated King James of England that he began to pressure the Dutch magistrates for the arrest of the criminals.

"Impossible," replied the Dutch, "since they are registered as students at the university, and as such must be accorded the immunity of regular students who will be punished by the curator of the university."

It was a shrewd way out, but it worked. It enabled the Pilgrims to continue their work uninterrupted, but they were not "home," and dissatisfaction remained.

"In their flight," commented E. G. White,

they had left their houses, their goods and their means of liveli-
hood. They were strangers in a strange land, among a people of
different language and customs. They were forced to resort to new
and untried occupations to earn their bread. Middle-aged men,
who had spent their lives tilling the soil, had now to learn
mechanical trades. . . . But they cheerfully accepted the situation
and lost no time in idleness or repining. Though often pinched
with poverty, they thanked God for the blessings which were still
granted them, and found their joy in unmolested spiritual com-
munion.[5]

History has shown that the Leiden magistrates were more than
justified in granting permission to the refugees to settle in their
city, because it states in the records approximately ten years later
that "these English people have now lived amongst us these ten
years and never any complaint or accusation has been brought
against any of them."

But their meager existence in Holland—even though wrought
amidst perfect religious freedom—finally led them to reexamine
their goals. Their colony had become quite popular with the
Separatists in England, and in just ten years the Leiden congregation had swelled to more than four hundred members, each
one trying to achieve success within the English-Dutch society.
But they clearly wanted more.

William Bradford complained,

For many of the children, that were of best dispositions and
gracious inclinations, haveing lernde to bear the yoake in their
youth, and willing to bear parte of their parents burden, were,
often times, so oppressed with their heavie labours, that though
their minds were free and willing, yet their bodies bowed under
the weight of the same, and became decreped in their early youth;
the vigor of nature being consumed in the very budd as it were.
But that which was more lamentable, and of all sorowed most
heavie to be borned, was that many of their children, by these
occasions, and the great licentiousness of youth in that countrie,
and the manifold temptations of the place, were drawne away by
evill examples into extravagante and dangerous courses, getting
the raines off their neks, and departing from their parents. Some

became souldiers, others tooke upon them farr viages by sea, and others some worse courses, tending to dissolutnes and the danger of their soules, to the greefe of their parents and dishonour to God. So that they saw their posteritie would be in danger to degenerate and be corrupted.

Lastly, (and which was not least), a great hope and inward zeall they had of laying some good foundation, or at least to make some way thereunto, for the propagating and advancing of the gospell of the kingdom of Christ in those remote parts of the world.[6]

These points have been emphasized over and over again as the paramount reasons for the Pilgrims' journey to the New World, but there were other, *political* issues that played as important a role. The Separatists, while still in England, must have been aware of the fact that the trade and religious war between Catholic Spain and what later became the United Netherlands had finally come to an end at Gibraltar on April 25, 1607, when the Dutch admiral Jacob van Heemskerk destroyed the Spanish fleet. This battle resulted in the signing of a peace treaty between Spain and the United Netherlands on April 9, 1609. Under this treaty the United Netherlands was to be recognized as a Protestant republic for initially a period of twelve years.

A mere two months prior to the signing of the peace treaty, the Pilgrims arrived. However, the threat of political uncertainty and the fear of a renewed invasion by Spain at the end of the twelve-year truce on April 9, 1621, definitely hastened the decision of the Pilgrims to move away from the Old World. In August 1620, nine months before the treaty's expiration date, they left for what they hoped would be safer havens. Bradford comments in his book *History of Plymouth Plantation,*

> The Indians could hardly be worse than the Spaniards, who, as soon as the truce ended, would attack the Netherlands and visit their utmost cruelty and displeasure upon those who had been calling Satan a Catholic for years.[7]

The spirit that spurred the Pilgrims' departure is not confined to the 120 documents we studied in the Municipal Archives in

Leiden. Just one hundred yards from the heavy oak door of the Pilgrim Fathers Museum where we did our research is the spot where the Fathers boarded the horse-drawn barges that transported them to Delfshaven. Leiden still throbs with Pilgrim nostalgia from the narrow cobblestone streets where they walked to the green moss-stained walls of the old canal and the Nonnenbrug (Nunsbridge) from which they departed.

A. G. A. Bachrach, Dutch Professor of English Literature and the Director of the Sir Thomas Browne Institute in Leiden, comments, "They left from their doorsteps, sailing in barges drawn by horses—the cheapest way of transport allowing the largest amount of luggage. Sometimes this was not very comfortable when storms arose on the lakes that had to be crossed, but one got there, and got there cheaply."[8]

After boarding the sixty-ton *Speedwell* lying in the harbor, the Pilgrims sailed to Southhampton and joined the larger *Mayflower*. Because of its unseaworthiness, the *Speedwell* was forced to turn back, leaving the *Mayflower* to sail alone to immortality.

How John Robinson, the religious spokesman and biblical scholar of the Pilgrims, must have agonized as the first gentle wisps of wind touched the sails of the barges, and he saw the *scheepsjager* horses pull the tiny ships through the murky waters of the canal and out of his sight! It had been agreed by the congregation that on this first trip to the unknown New World, William Brewster would lead the Pilgrims if they formed the smaller part of the Leiden congregation, and John Robinson would be the leader if they formed the greater part.

Interestingly enough, a larger group of the refugees chose *not* to leave the safe confines of Leiden. They had found freedom of religion and grumbled about having to move again. In his parting address to the voyagers, Robinson, well aware of this dissent, simply ignored it. There were greater issues at stake. He struggled to control his emotions as he addressed the hushed audience.

Brethren, we are now erelong part asunder, and the Lord knoweth whether I shall live to see your faces more. But whether the Lord hath appointed it or not, I charge you before God and His blessed angels to follow me no farther than I have followed Christ. If God should reveal anything to you by any other instrument of His, be as ready to receive it as ever you were to receive any truth of my ministry; for I am very confident the Lord hath more truth and light yet to break forth out of His holy word. . . .[9]

For my part, I cannot sufficiently bewail the condition of the reformed churches, who are come to a period in religion and will go at present no farther than the instruments of their reformation.[10]

Then Robinson added his most important words for a congregation who were soon to be split by the ocean waves:

Remember your church covenant, in which you have agreed to walk in all the ways of the Lord, made or to be made known unto you. *Remember* your promise and covenant with God and with one another, to receive whatever light and truth shall be made known unto you from His written word; *but withal, take heed, I beseech you,* what you receive for truth, and compare it and weigh it with other scriptures of truth before you accept it; for it is not possible the Christian world should come too lately out of such thick antichristian darkness, and that full perfection of knowledge should break forth at once.[11]

Bradford later wrote,

. . . Truly dolfull was the sight of that sade and mournful parting; to see what sight and sobbs and praires did sound amongst them, what tears did gush from every eye, and pithy speeches peirst each harte; that sundry of the Dutch strangers that stood on the key as spectators could not refraine from tears.[12]

And John Robinson stayed behind.

In some ways the years were lonely ones for Robinson in Leiden, for even though he had his congregation, they began to experience an overwhelming desire to cling to their faith and customs and be free from the influence of the Dutch. As a result, more of these people left Leiden to resettle across the Atlantic in

New Plymouth—while those who remained intermarried with the Hollanders, thus bringing about the dissolution of the congregation. On March 1, 1625, John Robinson died and found his resting place among the stones he loved—those of the stately walls of Leiden's St. Pieterskerk. Though the exact spot has been forgotten, a memorial to him still survives on the church wall.

A historic epoch had ended; a new one was about to begin.

Wanting to leave the past behind them and rebuild their lives was uppermost in the minds of the Pilgrims once they had settled in their new land. But the years spent in the United Netherlands had made an indelible impression on the group, and the spirit of republicanism appeared impossible to erase. The forms and institutions in which that republican spirit expressed itself in the United Netherlands had a resounding influence on the political development of the Pilgrims' way of life, and this Dutch heritage is more directly traceable in the framework of the American republic than are the institutions of monarchial England. Though we are English in speech, we are Dutch in institution to a much greater degree than is generally supposed.

Albert B. Osborn, who appraised this legacy shortly after World War I, listed many facets of this amazing heritage. They include:

- The equal division of the estates among surviving children
- A written constitution, one having existed in Holland since 1579 though still unfound in England
- The organization of the United States Senate, an elective body with a fixed equal representation for each state and an age qualification for membership
- Free schools
- Religious freedom
- The recording of title deeds
- The written ballot

- The assignment of counsel to poor defendants charged with crime
- The inability of the Executive to declare war without the consent of Congress[13]

All these features and many more had no parallel in England but clearly derived their inspiration from Dutch sources, placing a much greater importance on the "Leiden connection" than is often realized.

With the arrival of the Pilgrims in New Plymouth in 1620, the second permanent English settlement was established on the continent, the first one made at Jamestown, Virginia, in 1607. Some 155 years later, the turbulence of development, dissatisfaction, greed, and finally open revolt brought forth the American Revolution.

Much of America's early period has been recorded, but other segments, perhaps equally as important, are obscured by time. Such is the case with a story that first appeared in December 1880 in *National Tribune* and has been debated ever since. This paper, now known as the *Stars and Stripes*, tells a tale that critics would prefer to relegate to the realms of fantasy, while others, believing that the birth of the United States was in direct fulfillment of biblical prophecy, see in it a warning for the future. Reprinted in the *Stars and Stripes* issue of December 21, 1950, it is a stirring account of a vision revealed to George Washington of the future developments of America.

"The last time I ever saw Anthony Sherman was on the fourth of July, 1859, in Independence Square," writes Wesley Bradshaw, publisher of the *National Tribune*. "He was then ninety-nine years old, and becoming very feeble. But though so old, his dimming eyes rekindled as he gazed upon Independence Hall, which he had come to visit once more.

"'Let's go into the hall,'" he said, 'I want to tell you of an incident in Washington's life—one which no one alive knows of except myself; and if you live, you will before long see it verified. *Mark the prediction, you will see it verified.'"*

This is Sherman's tale as Bradshaw recorded it:

"From the opening of the Revolution we experienced all phases of fortune, now good and now ill, one time victorious and another conquered. The darkest period we had, I think, was when Washington, after several reverses, retreated to Valley Forge, where he resolved to pass the winter of 1777.

"Ah, I have often seen the tears coursing down our dear commander's care-worn cheeks, as he would be conversing with a confidential officer about the condition of his poor soldiers. You have doubtless heard the story of Washington going to the thicket to pray. Well, it was not only true, but he used to pray in secret for aid and comfort. And God brought us safely through the darkest days of tribulation.

"One day, I remember it well, the chilly winds whispered through the leafless trees, though the sky was cloudless and the sun shone brightly. He remained in his quarters nearly all the afternoon, alone. When he came out I noticed that his face was a shade paler than usual, and there seemed to be something on his mind of more than ordinary importance. Returning just after dusk, he dispatched an orderly to the quarters of an officer, who was presently in attendance. After a preliminary conversation of about half an hour, Washington, gazing upon his companion with that strange look of dignity which he alone could command, said to the latter,

"'I do not know whether it is owing to the anxiety of my mind, or what, but this afternoon, as I was sitting at this table engaged in preparing a dispatch, something in the apartment seemed to disturb me. Looking up I beheld standing opposite me a singularly beautiful being. So astonished was I, for I had given strict orders not to be disturbed, that it was some moments before I found language to inquire the cause of the visit. A second, a third, and even a fourth time did I repeat the question, but received no answer from my mysterious visitor except a slight raising of the eyes.

"'By this time I felt strange sensations spreading over me. I would have risen but the riveted gaze of the being before me rendered volition impossible. I assayed once more to speak but my tongue had become useless, as if paralyzed. A new influence, mysterious, potent, irresistible, took possession of me. All I could do was to gaze steadily, vacantly, at my unknown visitor.

"'Gradually the surrounding atmosphere seemed to fill with sensations, and grew luminous. Everything about me seemed to rarify, the mysterious visitor also becoming more airy and yet more distinct to my eyes than before. I began to feel as one dying, or rather to experience the sensations which I have sometimes imagined accompany death. I did not think, I did not reason, I did not move. All were alike impossible. I was only conscious of gazing fixedly, vacantly at my companion.

"'Presently I heard a voice saying, "Son of the Republic, Look and Learn," while at the same time my visitor extended an arm eastward.

"'I now beheld a heavy white vapor at some distance rising fold upon fold. This gradually dissipated, and I looked upon a strange scene. Before me lay, spread out in one vast plain all the countries of the world—Europe, Asia, Africa and America. I saw rolling and tossing between Europe and America the billows of the Atlantic and between Asia and America lay the Pacific. "Son of the Republic," said the same mysterious voice as before, "Look and Learn."

"'At that moment I beheld a dark shadowy being like an angel, standing or rather floating in mid-air between Europe and America. Dipping water out of the ocean in the hollow of each hand, he sprinkled some upon America with his right hand, while with his left he cast some over Europe. Immediately a cloud arose from these countries and joined in mid-ocean. For a while it seemed stationary, and then it moved slowly westward until it enveloped America in its murky folds. Sharp flashes of lightning gleamed through it at intervals, and I heard the smothered groans and cries of the American people.

"'A second time the angel dipped from the ocean and sprinkled it out as before. The dark cloud was then drawn back to the ocean in whose heaving billows it sank from view.

"'A third time I heard the mysterious voice saying, "Son of the Republic, Look and Learn." I cast my eyes upon America and beheld villages and towns and cities springing up one after another until the whole land from the Atlantic to the Pacific was dotted with them. Again I heard the mysterious voice saying, "Son of the Republic, the end of the century cometh, look and learn."

"'And this time the dark shadowy angel turned his face southward. From Africa I saw an ill-omened spectre approach our land. It flitted slowly and heavily over every town and city of the latter. The inhabitants presently set themselves in battle array against each other. As I continued looking I saw a bright angel on whose brow rested a crown of light on which was traced the word "Union." He was bearing the American flag. He placed the flag between the divided nation and said, "Remember, ye are brethren."

"'Instantly, the inhabitants, casting down their weapons, became friends once more and united around the National Standard.

"'Again I heard the mysterious voice saying, "Son of the Republic, Look and Learn." At this the dark shadowy angel placed a trumpet to his mouth and blew three distinct blasts; and taking water from the ocean, he sprinkled it upon Europe, Asia and Africa.

"'Then my eyes beheld a fearful scene. From each of these continents arose thick black clouds that were soon joined into one. And through this mass there gleamed a dark red light by which I saw hordes of armed men. These men, moving with the cloud, marched by land and sailed by sea to America, which country was enveloped in the volume of the cloud. And I dimly saw these vast armies devastate the whole country and burn the villages, towns and cities which I had seen springing up.

"'As my ears listened to the thundering of the cannon, clash-ing of swords and the shouts and cries of millions in mortal combat, I again heard the mysterious voice saying, "Son of the Republic, Look and Learn." When this voice had ceased, the dark shadowy angel placed his trumpet once more to his mouth and blew a long and fearful blast.

"'Instantly a light as of a thousand suns shone down from above me and pierced and broke into fragments the dark cloud which enveloped America. At the same moment the angel upon whose head still shown the words "Union" and who bore our national flag in one hand and a sword in the other, descended from the heavens attended by legions of white spirits. These immediately joined the inhabitants of America who I perceived were well-nigh overcome but who, immediately taking courage again, closed up their broken ranks and renewed the battle.

"'Again, amid the fearful noise of the conflict I heard the mysterious voice saying, "Son of the Republic, Look and Learn." As the voice ceased, the shadowy angel for the last time dipped water from the ocean and sprinkled it upon America. Instantly the dark cloud rolled back, together with the armies it had brought, leaving the inhabitants of the land victorious.

"'Then once more I beheld the villages, towns and cities spr-inging up where I had seen them before, while the bright angel, planting the azure standard he had brought in the midst of them, cried with a loud voice,

"'"While the stars remain, and the heavens send down dew upon the earth, so long shall the Union last." And taking from his brow the crown on which blazoned the word "Union," he placed it upon the standard while the people kneeling down said, "Amen."

"'The scene instantly began to fade and dissolve, and I at last saw nothing but the rising, curling vapor I at first beheld. This also disappeared, and I found myself once more gazing upon the mysterious visitor, who, in the same voice I had heard before, said,

"""*Son of the Republic, what you have seen is thus interpreted. Three great perils will come upon the Republic. The most fearful for her is the third. But the whole world united shall not prevail against her. Let every child of the Republic learn to live for his God, his land and Union.*" With these words the vision vanished, and I started from my seat and felt that I had seen a vision wherein had been shown me the birth, the progress and destiny of the United States . . .'" [italics ours].[14]

It was not until several years later, in 1781, that the last battle of the American Revolution was fought. Another two years expired before the final peace treaty with England had been signed, giving America its independence. It was indeed an occasion fitting the beginning of the vision, for it was not only the first armed American conflict, but one involving European nations as well. The second half of the nineteenth century found the United States engaged in a needless civil war, the end result being a renewed union around the national standard—in agreement with the second part of the vision.

While this controversial vision does not indicate the probable causes for the third conflict, identified as "the most fearful," it certainly has all the implications of a conflict of major proportions—a war to be fought on American soil. Even though this nation has been an active participant in several international conflicts, war itself is not part of its birthright. America was not born in tribal hostility as were many other nations, but its birth was the result of a confrontation over principles—a set of values to be considered eternal. America as a nation is indeed unprecedented in human history, and undoubtedly much of its success lies in the Constitution's acceptance of the biblical view of the nature of man. In fact, the Founding Fathers' perception of man was already described by Jeremiah: "The heart is deceitful above all things, and desperately wicked: who can know it?" (Jer. 17:9).

Is it perhaps a renewed struggle over the value and global application of these "founding" principles that will plunge

America into this final "most fearful" conflict? Or can it be due to a diminishing emphasis on these principles within our culture? The rise of America has been a phenomenon without equal in history; will its decline also be as spectacular?

It is a difficult task to state with any absolute assurance why cultures have to rise and decay, yet they do. The notable civilizations of the past such as Egypt, Greece, and Rome are no longer great. Their eminence has faded, leaving only memories of their accomplishments. For years experts have debated with one another as to precisely why Rome, Egypt, or any prominent civilization of the past fell. Certainly any generalization concerning cultural decay, however sophisticated and supported with facts, is open to serious challenge.

Yet the simple fact remains that *cultures do decay,* and reasons can be found that, if not totally then at least in large measure, account for why they do. Unique factors are attributable for certain cultures decaying at particular times; however, a single fact emerges—that cultures destroy themselves starting from the inside as surely as anything can be stated with historical certainty. Furthermore, it is a curious fact that the decay of cultures is much like the performance of a drunken man: he insists he is doing better precisely to the extent that his actual behavior is degenerating from intoxication. Hence, *one ought to suspect that at the moment when cultures primarily concern themselves with progress and hope, there is hidden in this concern the implicit awareness, however slight, that things are not well at all.*

Does our hoping indicate that something has gone wrong and this is why we must hope? In today's America, the post-Watergate euphoria is indeed suspicious. It is much like the proverbial boy whistling as he passes the graveyard. These are troubled times, and it is quite possible that Watergate has shown us not only *how* the system works, but more importantly *that* the system works. Quite simply, as Charles Colson had the courage to assert in *Born Again,* Watergate was both a symptom and a product of moral decay.[15] This decay begins slowly, but then at a very rapid rate corrodes the basic fiber of civilization until there is no possibility of repair. And as Watergate has shown us, people can hang on until the final possible moment, believing in their own deluded way that nothing is really fundamentally wrong. Yet America is in trouble, and it is fundamental. Furthermore, as with all great civilizations of the past, this moral decay is evident if we will only muster the courage to look.

It is apparent that American history is embedded in the larger context of Western civilization and follows an evolutionary line of cultural growth. The United States epitomizes the extreme position that mere change is progress and that despite particular problems, things are getting better. Indeed, is it not the case that, as one of America's technological giants would have it, "Progress is our most important product"? And even though we have problems, are we not confident that their solution will inevitably be achieved? Is this very optimism, the American "great hope," just a mask for despair, an implicit awareness that we have fallen far short of the dream and that perhaps the dream itself is becoming a nightmare?

While unanimity was somewhat lacking among the Founding Fathers, they did nevertheless share a faith in both God and reason that were to be the building blocks of the nation. It was from the Greeks that they appropriated the concept of reason as both a liberating force and the mechanism for progress. As Thomas Paine determined in his *Rights of Man*, progress was almost inevitable given the proper application of reason to the solution of basic human problems.[16] It was as if society were a giant machine, fashioned perfectly by its Creator, needing only careful maintenance by its cultural mechanics to ensure perfect functioning. Society as a flawless machine was to be the vehicle of human happiness. America would be in magnitude what the august Greek city of Athens was but in miniature. "Reason" was to be the key that would unlock the secrets of the societal machine as it would unlock the laws of nature, for as Paine assuredly believed, "All great laws of society are laws of nature."[17]

Of course, the appeal to reason as a guiding force for action was recognized to be ultimately impotent unless properly applied. Also, the Founding Fathers obviously recognized that as Greece surely fell to the conquering Romans, America would fall to its future "Romans" unless this reason was properly employed in the service of God. The societal machine as created by man could function only insofar as its rules and regulations were modeled after the universe created in its perfection by God. America was to be a truly Christian nation and, unlike Greece, would survive as long as Christian precepts guided the reasoning of its citizens.

Exactly what would it mean for America to claim the title "Christian nation"? After all, some would argue that respect for America's religious freedom at least implies the liberty to choose any religion, including non-Christian religions, or not to be religious at all. The Founding Fathers were wise enough to recognize that a total separation between church and state is required if religious faith is to be freely sought and believed. Yet there is no doubt that the necessity for such faith was to be the distinctive characteristic of America and the basis for the assurance that the United States, unlike other nations, would not fall but survive as God's great warning beacon to other, less-favored countries. *America was to be God's chosen nation, and her people were to have God on their side.*

In studying religion, social scientists distinguish between particular religions in America and the more general phenomenon of simple religious belief. One does not have to be a social scientist, however, to perceive that the beliefs and practices have always been diverse and complex, yet not one of them merged with the ideology of the men who formed this nation. Their plans did not make allowance for denominational interaction with government, and because of this, America is a land without any attachment to a particular religious group.

Concerning religion in general, however, social scientists cannot find a dividing line between religion and government.

They have identified a strong religious foundation underlying American culture, and this foundation has been judged to be basic and inviolate.

Robert Bellah has coined a phrase often used when referring to this religion foundation: "civil religion."[18] By this he means a passionate, fundamental belief in God that lies at the very heart of the American system. According to Bellah, this belief is not restricted to any religious denomination, but is more sympathetic to fundamental Protestantism.

President Dwight D. Eisenhower referred to this spirituality in saying, "Our government makes no sense unless it is founded in a deeply felt religious faith—and I don't care what it is."[19] This statement may sound a bit extreme, since just *any* religious faith is not what Americans generally mean when they claim belief in God; but it shows the insistence that, for many, belief and trust in God are as American as the Fourth of July.

Herein lies the basis of America's civil religion. Matters of personal religious conviction, patterns of personal worship, and choices of church and synagogue attendance are private decisions guaranteed by the Bill of Rights; and they cannot be violated by government interference. The common belief in God shared by the majority of Americans, however, is integral to the American system and is *the* guiding force of the state—at least in the intentions of our Founding Fathers.

Accepting this "guiding force" in national affairs really means that democracy as the simple will of the people cannot be regarded as the ultimate force in politics. Rather, the will of the people is itself under judgment by a still higher power. That power is God.

When taking the oath of office, many American presidents make an appeal to God, and Bellah, upon analyzing this, has discovered it to be an inseparable part of American history.

Referring specifically to President John F. Kennedy's inaugural address but in terms that apply generally to all American presidents, Bellah notes,

The whole address can be understood as only the most recent statement of a theme that lies very deep in the American tradition, namely the obligation, both collective and individual, to carry out God's will on earth. This was the motivating spirit of those who founded America, and it has been present in every generation since.[20]

It is evident that throughout its history this country's leaders have adhered to the idea that America is to be judged by the power upon which her destiny rests—the power of God. There is no doubt that in essence America is rooted in a belief in God and that her actions as a nation are to be judged in an ultimate sense *beyond* the mere criteria of apparent prosperity and material success.

What then can be said of America in the decade just past?

Has she matured in the light of divine guidance? Has God's work on earth truly become her own? Or, has America, like many other past civilizations, sprouted within her very own soul the seeds of her destruction? Is it possible that she has willfully averted her eyes from the Guiding Light that nourished her soul and made her a moral giant among the nations of this earth?

Chapter Two

An Anxious Nation

It is a curious fact that the tremendous technological achievements and obvious material advantages of modern America are but surface phenomena, obscuring serious, cancerous processes that gnaw at her very being. Nowhere in this country is this process more evident than in what we might want to call the "mental health" of the nation. Clearly, a nation inhabited by troubled, disturbed people cannot really be called "great." It is assumed that a country's greatness should be reflected in its citizenry; yet, if there is one single characteristic of modern America that stands out above all else, it is that the United States has become dominated not by persons seeing themselves

as children of God, but rather by the distressed and troubled who
have misguidedly convinced themselves that they have finally
matured into what psychologist Phillip Rieff has called "psychological man."[1]

What and who is this "psychological man"?

Professionals in psychology describe him as a being who believes himself to be a self-sufficient person, unattached to any
particular ideology, and certainly not "under" any absolute belief
system. God, if believed in at all, is functionalized. He may be
useful in troubled times, it is reasoned, but certainly no sacrifices
need to be made to Him or for Him. Psychological man advocates a "do-your-own-thing" philosophy and submits to a new
kind of spiritual healer who holds doctoral degrees and shuns
speaking of sin or real guilt. "What one does is not the problem,"
he says, "only the guilt feelings for doing what is done are the
problem." As the American Psychiatric Association would have
it, homosexuality itself is not a sickness, but a person's negative
feelings about his homosexuality are indicators of a "disease."
And the treatment they are likely to prescribe is to overcome the
negative feelings. This is a curious twist of logic and reasoning
that characterizes modern America. It has been said that beliefs
must be judged by their fruits. If this is true, then what assessment do we give of modern "psychological man"?

Otto Friedrich has irritated social scientists by analyzing what
Americans seem to be doing best, and that is, for him, *Going
Crazy*—the title of his recent book. If there is one thing that can
be said with assurance, Friedrich writes, it is that the average
American citizen has emerged within the context of mental
health as an individual whose "normal" state of affairs is being
mentally ill! Consider a few figures gleaned from Friedrich's
book:[2]

America has 337 state and county mental hospitals into which
more than 400,000 people were admitted in 1974. And admissions are increasing at a staggering rate. Add to this more than
90,000 people admitted to 156 private clinics (1971 figures), and

there are perhaps half a million individuals literally "going crazy" each year. Well over 800 of every 100,000 persons in the United States are admitted to mental hospitals *yearly*. According to Friedrich's data, more than 1.7 million Americans reside in the hospitals for the insane. Furthermore, 4 million persons are treated for mental problems apart from hospital confinement, giving a conservative estimate of 1,982 per 100,000 of persons treated for insanity or mental illness, roughly 2 percent of the United States population.

Yet these thought-provoking statistics tell only half the story. Friedrich has also pointed out that if drug-related mental problems are added, the figures rise tremendously. For instance, there are approximately 100,000 officially recognized drug addicts in America and many more unrecognized ones. Similarly there are at least 9 million alcoholics in America! Obviously, it is *drugs and not religion* that has become the "opiate" of the people!

And if the above-mentioned statistics aren't depressing enough, we still must consider that in 1972, some 18,880 murders were meticulously recorded by the Justice Department. And while it is abundantly clear that Americans continue to kill one another in great numbers, they kill themselves even more frequently. In 1972, for direct comparison with the murder count, 17,290 males and 6,980 females ended their own lives, a total of 24,270 persons: a figure based on official statistics that many social scientists believe accounts for only one-tenth of the actual number. Moreover, the ultimate irony of suicide is that it is most prevalent among the successful; and to compound the paradox even further, medical doctors—and especially psychiatrists— head the list.

Because of America's troubled population, massive government resources and efforts have been directed toward relieving mental pressures on the nation by guiding as many people as possible into various therapy programs. The National Institute of Mental Health has become a colossal governmental agency attesting to the central role of madness in modern America. Yet still another irony remains, for while many are driven or pushed into therapy, evidence showing the effectiveness of the therapy programs has yet to be provided. Studies conducted by psychologist H. J. Eysenck[3] have repeatedly revealed that patients who receive official therapies are no better off than those who receive no therapy at all! In addition, other studies indicate that while some persons dramatically improve with psychotherapy, just as many *get worse* as a result of therapy. Thus, while mental and emotional imbalance perhaps characterizes much of America's "psychological man," the substantial use of psychotherapy as a treatment remains unjustified. One may hopefully believe that a "miracle cure" for the ills of the nation lies in the future, but at the same time such claims belie the fundamental issue that sin, not sickness, lies at the heart of America's confused populace. Even the distinguished psychiatrist Karl Menninger wondered about this point, titling one of his most popular works *Whatever Became of Sin?*[4]

It is a well-documented fact that much of what is labeled mental illness today was formerly recognized in more straightforward terminology as "sin." Sin therefore had the advantage of being easily identified by both lay and professional persons, rooted as it was in deviation from standards identified with America's great religious tradition. Hence people who sinned were to be brought back into the fold, to be "saved," and the criterion was at least in principle clear—an awareness that only a holy life is a happy life. Yet the emergence of psychological language changed all this. Now, what once was "sin" became known as "liberated behavior," and many actions once thought sinful became "ill." Alcoholism became a "disease," and a cure was sought in secular therapies. Value judgments were not acceptable, and alcoholics, being merely passive victims of a "disease," were not to be held responsible for their behavior. Individuals had to be treated rather than punished and institutions arose to handle "illnesses" ranging from drug abuse through depression to murder and attempted suicide. More and more people were identified as needing treatment, thereby "preventing" illness by diagnosing it in its earliest stages. Yet, as sins become identified as "illnesses," more sickness is discovered until the distinction between healthy and ailing people is almost negligible.

In the now-famous Manhattan Study,[5] a group of distinguished social scientists investigated a random sample of inhabitants of New York's Midtown Manhattan, searching for the presence of yet undetected psychiatric symptoms. Of the 1,660 adults studied in some detail, only 18.5 percent were found to be "well" and free from psychiatric symptoms. The vast majority (81.5 percent) were found to suffer from some degree of psychiatric impairment. Furthermore, approximately three-fourths of these people had never sought any form of professional help. This was the case even though nearly 3 percent of the "not well" persons were identified as "incapacitated" and almost 8 percent of them were identified as having "severe symptom" formation. In addition, while the degree of seriousness of illness varied, the majority of the ill persons had more than merely "mild" symptom formation. Hence, in one of the most carefully designed and massive surveys of a contemporary American city, the conclusion reached by social scientists was clear—*the majority of New York's inhabitants were non-hospitalized but psychiatrically ill individuals!* Dare we say, "As New York goes, so goes the nation"?

But other studies are even more revealing.

If the majority of people in America's largest metropolis might be considered by psychological studies to be less than well, what about those who are already committed? The "state of the art" of psychiatry is not half as exact as its proponents would like us to believe. At least this is one implication of the study conducted by David L. Rosenhan entitled "On Being Sane in Insane Places."[6]

Rosenhan devised a very simple experiment to test the ability of mental health personnel to diagnose mental illness. He selected "pseudo-patients"—persons who were not and never had been mentally ill. Among those "patients" were medical doctors, psychologists, and lay persons. Their instructions were to call mental hospitals and describe symptoms that were not characteristic of mental illness. The task given the pseudo-patients was quite simple: to see whether they would be admitted into a mental hospital, and then immediately to try to secure their release. The results of the first phase of this study were impressive but startling. *Everyone was admitted*—in many types of mental hospitals in widely scattered locations. Most of the "patients" were diagnosed as severely ill, primarily "schizophrenic." After an average stay of 129 days in the hospital, all were discharged, not as "cured" but rather as having their illness in "remission." Furthermore, for these pseudo-patients, the average amount of medication administered during their confinement was no less than 2,100 pills! *As a final irony, while mental health personnel in the hospitals saw these normal, sane persons as sick, the truly ill inhabitants of these hospitals recognized these pseudo-patients as normal!*

The mental health establishment was shocked when Rosenhan's research was first published. It argued against the validity of the study, assuring Rosenhan that they could reliably detect mental illness and that his data were not typical. Whether this battery of official criticism evoked a smile or a frown from Rosenhan, we do not know; however, he did counteract in a strong way by launching a reversal study. *He announced in advance* that he was placing pseudo-patients and regular admission patients in various mental hospitals, and the mental health personnel were warned that they would once more be evaluated. Their task was to be "on guard" and to identify the patients who in fact were well.

Rosenhan's work again produced astounding results. While mental health personnel *could* agree that there were indeed pseudo-patients, they *could not* agree among themselves precisely who the pseudo-patients were! Furthermore, the ultimate irony of the entire study was that Rosenhan announced that *no* pseudo-patients had been placed in the regular admissions at all! Thus, the combined results of the two Rosenhan studies were devastating. He proved that not only can mental health personnel confuse normal people with the insane when normal persons are placed among the ill, but when warned to identify "hidden" well persons among the ill, the personnel misidentified ill persons as normal.

Confusing?

It certainly was to the mental health establishment, for it severely attacked the credibility of its leadership. Their skill in distinguishing ill from well was suspect, as were their distinctions between being "well" and being "mentally ill." As Robert Coles, an eminent psychiatrist, has stated,

> Exactly *what*, if anything, is "mental health"? Who is "mentally ill"—as opposed to the rest of us, who make do, if not prosper psychologically? Is the whole subject of "mental health" a phantom—a means by which different people, possessed of different notions about life and its purposes, turn on one another categorically, morally, and even, it can be said, politically? I am "healthy" (good, saved, favored by God or fate) and you are an outcast of sorts?[7]

That mental health personnel are confused concerning the psychological health of the nation is readily apparent. It is a problem basic to the social science disciplines. Their effort to construct value-free definitions of health are caught in the paradox that "health" itself is a value term, for no two "experts" can agree on the meaning of the word. The nature of "the good life" and "the whole person" are purely ethical concepts and must be rooted in some ethical system. Within the great American tradition, that ethical system is based on God and His unfolding of history, particularly that of the United States. Hence a system for healing the nation's maladies outside of God's plan is an illusion and a vain effort to deny the reality of sin and evil.

Not surprisingly, we learn that most psychiatrists and psychologists involved in "helping" others are avowedly anti-religious.

They are secular priests operating in a world devoid of theological guidance. In fact, the rapid acceptance of basic Freudian ideas came largely in response to a religious system of healing that emerged in the eighteenth century and was considered to be a threat to the medical establishment.[8] As a result, we have become a nation, rooted in a belief in God, literally going crazy as it departs further and further from notions of sin, seeking salvation in an impotent secular priesthood.

The moral decay of America from within seems verified in the psychiatric and psychological confusion that surrounds current efforts to confront the massive rise in "mental health problems." We are literally beginning to experience the mental breakdown of a nation.[9] America is on center stage, decaying from within, while an anxious world watches. The internal problems of its inhabitants reflect and affirm the decline of previous civilizations that stubbornly refused to recognize their own demise.

What causes this decay amid such obvious wealth and "progress?" What has happened to America? We must look at our country in light of the great goals of the Founding Fathers before we can judge whether there really has been "progress" or just changes indicative of degeneration and national decay.

It is noteworthy that many modern social scientists are accepting a model of man and society that closely parallels an evangelical Christian perspective. What is more surprising is that even such apparently antireligious geniuses as Freud seem to have had essentially Christian elements in their thought. Clearly Christianity has taught us that a person's salvation does not lead him to a better existence in this world. Tainted with sin, humanity cannot create a perfect world within which to perfect itself. Whatever we do is usually only an improvement of the state of things caused by the Fall. While social constraints and controls are necessary and can serve to limit the individual's innovative sinfulness to some extent, the Christian ultimately recognizes that at best the task is to control one's basic nature and to seek salvation in acknowledgment of a power greater than himself. Here then lies the moral foundation of America as a Christian nation, for her "civil religion" assures judgment by a greater power—by almighty God.

This basic Christian model assures us that we have a dual nature. We are sinful beings, products of the Fall and capable of great evil and wrongdoings. This contradicts modern humanistic theories which tend to argue that all will be well if we are simply allowed to grow in a free and permissive environment, unfettered by "unnecessary controls"—especially religious moral codes. But this absurd view cannot prevail against the obvious fact that realizing basic potentials includes recognizing the existence of evil and wrongdoing. Hence, permissiveness, instead of freeing man, creates additional evil and sin in the world due precisely to the "liberation" of much of a person's evil nature, thus adding to the complexities of life in Western society.

Christian perspective adds another dimension to us and our nature. True, we are rooted in original sin, but it is also true that salvation is available if we will only believe and follow absolute principles whose purpose is to bind us so that we can be free. This "binding" inhibits the unlimited expression of our evil nature and places us under the guidance of God. Individuals can reject this constraint, but they do so on their own responsibility. When many people reject God's guidance, the reaction is compounded and it begins to affect the national welfare of the state.

The social scientist who studies our modern society is highly unlikely to use Christian terms when expressing theories. Yet, it is a strange and unexplainable fact that when most social theories are stripped to their bare essentials, they are very similar to a basic Christian model. Somehow, no matter how drastically we attempt to undermine the godly foundation underlying a nation such as ours, flurries of Christian principles keep drifting through the conflicting philosophies influencing our development.

The psychoanalyst Sigmund Freud is often cited as the psychological genius who ushered in the permissive era. And it is strange that the theories of Freud, who actually detested the

United States, met with such wide acceptance in this country. Renowned as opposing religious thought and urging atheism as a modern "enlightened" alternative, Freud curiously enough argued that man's nature is powerfully corrupt—a concept similar to that found in Christianity. He contended that the unsocialized, uncivilized person is dominated by a tendency to demand immediate gratification of basic needs, and this demand compels individuals to aggress against one another in order to find satisfaction. To this Freud added the "superego," the conscience which, according to him, acts as a brake on this demand for gratification. Both Freud and Christianity insist that only with a moral dimension—a moral sense, so to speak—could mankind achieve true greatness. Similarily the nation with the greatest moral sense—the nation with a belief in true and absolute principles derived from God—will be favored.

This, of course, is what the Founding Fathers intended for America. It is no secret to anyone who has drawn comparisons between Freud and Christian teachings that Freud rejected the basic Christian message; yet, they see in Freud an attempt to confront their own truths with a secular system of beliefs. Man *needs* a highly developed moral sense in order to construct within national boundaries the most nearly perfect nation possible. Only a country that is so directed can be truly great, and any deviation from such a standard signifies a move in the direction of progressive decay.

Is this what is happening in the United States today?

If we recognize the insights of Freud with respect to the necessity of moral constraint for the development of human greatness, then we can also recognize the role of morality in greatness.

In an influential book entitled *The Lonely Crowd*, David Riesman suggests that all societies have essentially two characteristics or problems.[10] The first one is being looked upon as some kind of management problem—with each new child presenting both a promise and a threat. The promise is that they too shall mature and continue the cultural traditions of their parents;

the threat is that they represent a challenge to any established system of morality in that they can undermine the moral system of the society and establish a new order of their own. Because of this, parents must transmit to their offspring the appropriate moral codes of their society; thus, the family as a social institution is society's first link to national greatness. Furthermore, as the family disintegrates, so will society.

The second problem, according to Riesman, concerns the technique of social control that is to be used. Recognizing that individuals *can* go wrong, all societies must be prepared to utilize techniques of social control for their straying members. And from the social scientists we learn a very important fact: *No society survives by the mere use of force to control deviant members.* Force by definition is ineffective in at least three ways: (1) It requires careful monitoring of behavior so that deviance can be detected; hence, persons quickly learn to become deviant and to violate cultural codes in situations where they cannot be readily detected; (2) force applied as punishment must be escalated to fit the crime; if someone robs a bank of $5,000, a fine of that amount or less would certainly not be deemed an effective deterrent; (3) most people are able to resist this kind of physical force.

"How then are people controlled?" we wonder. "What is the mechanism of social control that can lead a nation to greatness?"

The answer is plain: *It is the social character of its citizens.* Societies must create the character types that adhere to the values of the culture and in doing so transmit them to their children. Thus a strong family with cultural values rears its offspring to go forth and found similar strong families. A nation aspiring to moral greatness must have within its boundaries those striving for greatness themselves. Ultimately a country's character is but a reflection of its citizens, and its social control must have a foundation in basic personality characteristics for the majority of the people. If that is not the case, society will decay from within and become a life that is, as the often-quoted philosopher Thomas Hobbes would say, "solitary, poor, nasty, brutish, and short."

Riesman has concluded that the history of mankind is largely the history of cultures that have managed to instill in their citizens the values and accepted standards deemed necessary for survival. But this same history also shows the decay and degeneration of cultures. There is no doubt that cultures have destroyed themselves from within over and over again, simply because their members deviated from the very norms and standards of behavior that could have guaranteed their survival.

Times have changed.

In years past, traditions were firmly established within the various civilizations, and because contacts between cultures with different values were limited, there was not much impetus for change. Each culture functioned as a separate unit with its own moral codes, developing its own "traditional" values. Only one system of values was recognized as "right," and banishment befell the violators.

Centuries passed and civilizations "progressed." The interchange of ideas and concepts between different cultures has become an accepted fact. Using shame or banishment as a reason for exclusion from a group is no longer in vogue; these have lost their meaning. Now there's always another group to join. The disapproval of members of one group toward a deviant may simply compel the radical to move on to another, ultimately adopting the values of this new society.

Shame as the major controlling factor in society eventually gave way to guilt. But now guilt too is being undermined along America's passage to sophistication. Today we are often taught under the misguided influence of social science that "guilt is a bad thing" or, worse, guilt is an illusion. In fact, many of the therapies advocated and aimed at adjusting the "maladjusted" are directed precisely toward removing guilt feelings, as if they are the real problem. It is the conviction of guilt which assures the development of moral character. And it is this highly developed morality which forms the basis for America's civil religion and the underlying structure for its existence as a nation of Christian values.

The psychologists appear to be the victors.

Both shame and guilt are rapidly disappearing as mechanisms of social control and character development in today's United States. How far we have drifted from the original norms was the focal point of a Bicentennial Essay in *Time* magazine by James Q. Wilson, Professor of Government at Harvard University.[11] His article traces some aspects of the history of crime in America, and he reminds us that on the eve of the American Revolution, many of the colonists openly worried that a total political upheaval would unleash waves of crime and violence within the colonies, leaving only chaos in its wake. However, the anticipated "crime wave" was notably absent both during and after the Revolution; in fact, the phenomenon of widespread crime did not plague America until modern times. Crime in early America was rather sparse, and the modern notion of a police force and a prison system were unthinkable. It is as if the terms "progress" and "crime" are synonymous.

To say that our ancestors were all Puritans having an unerring sense of honesty and no faults would be a ludicrous assumption. Yet, years ago, Americans had a stronger moral sense, rooted in fundamental faith, uniformly taken as an appropriate guiding light for both individuals and society as a whole. Deviance was largely religious and moral and seldom violent. Living was generally directed toward fulfilling God's purposes as reflected in the newly emerging nation. In his *Time* essay Wilson notes that in seven densely populated counties of Massachusetts, more people were convicted for missing church services or for fornication on Sunday than were convicted of theft!

In those colonial days, banishment from the community was a most severe punishment. Not only would the guilty parties be totally isolated, but exile presented a threat to their very survival, for there was no assurance whatever that the offenders would be accepted in another settlement. The pillory, too, served as a deterrent. Control of crime was accomplished by systematic manipulation of reputation by the community.

But as America changed technologically, communities grew and diversified—and with change came greater tolerance for violation of established norms. Historians still can't quite agree on the reasons for this. Deviant behaviors were legitimized in new and growing liberal environments, and with the unyielding force of ocean waves, crime followed. The connection between the two is difficult to prove, yet the obvious fact remains that once a certain act is condoned, its frequency is assured.

Once America had yielded to this force, new techniques of crime prevention were required. And as the population in America increased, so did the diversification of values and beliefs. It was easy for advocates of a deviant act to find a group to support and legitimize it, and instead of reacting in positive ways, America tried to control the country's crumbling morality with violent measures. The need for a professional police force became quite apparent in the Boston riots of 1837. Modeled after the London police, the job of these unarmed individuals was to enforce rules agreed upon by the majority of the citizens. However, after another riot, the police were authorized by legislative action to carry weapons and were then armed as a matter of course. At this point, shame was no longer a relevant factor in dealing with punishment. Control of deviance had become a secular matter, administered by professionals using brute force.

Toddling America had now placed her first firm step in a direction from which there was no retreat.

This was only the beginning. A new institution, the prison system, was introduced to handle the deviants, now known as "criminals." Confinement replaced the pillory in the town square, and "penitentiaries"—places where criminals were forced to "repent"—became the center of the supposedly rehabilitative process. As an ultimate irony, these prisons became "schools for crime" in which offenders began to learn from other inmates how to perfect their criminal techniques. True rehabilitation was never really part of the system.

The obvious effect of all this was that communities, loosed from their firm roots in commonly shared values, adrift from God, lost their powers and ceased to be self-regulating. Wilson concludes in his Bicentennial Essay:

> For a long time and to our great disadvantage, we clung to the myth that there was a bureaucratic and governmental alternative to familial and communal virtue, that what parents, neighbors, and friends had failed to do, patrolmen, wardens, counselors and psychiatrists could provide. We struggled to maintain the hope that the police and schools could prevent crime and that prisons and treatment programs could rehabilitate criminals.
>
> We were wrong. We are coming to the unhappy realization that the police can rarely prevent crime and can solve at best only a small fraction of offenses. We now know that prisons cannot rehabilitate offenders. Hundreds of experimental studies on the treatment of criminals reach the same conclusion: no matter what form rehabilitation takes—vocational or academic training, individual or group counseling, long or short sentences, probation or parole—it does not work. We must finally concede that it is naive to suppose we can take a convict who has devoted a good part of his life to misbehavior of every sort and transform his character.[12]

There is little doubt that Wilson has isolated the real issue. The problem of both crime and nonconformity is truly a moral issue that has its roots in character development. A nation that fails to develop a highly principled population and instead becomes a land inhabited by morally insensitive people is a culture that is doomed to decay. These individuals who lack sufficient moral character cannot be controlled by mere social means. But it is also true that the alternative to labeling people criminals has been to brand them as needing professional mental health treatment. So it is here that we drift back into the sphere of religion. Somehow this incongruous trio—crime, mental illness, and religion—cannot be separated.

Mental illness *cannot* be set apart from religious belief, not because religious fanaticism often causes mental illness, but rather in the sense that all mental problems are fundamentally religious problems. Anton T. Boisen suggests that many of our mental problems are caused by our inability to come to grips with religious faith.[13] If this is true, then the treatment of nonconformists and the mentally ill outside of a religious context is doomed to fail.

Now the final question slowly surfaces: If America does not encourage shame and guilt as measures to govern social behavior, then what *does* she encourage?

The answer can be found in one word: Anxiety.

Riesman found that in complex societies, persons often fail to feel shame or guilt, and as a result a "do-your-own-thing" philosophy emerges. However, as more and more divergent groups appear, individuals begin to feel the need to belong to at least one of them. They focus attention on the changing fashions and trends and adapt their behavior and thoughts accordingly.

This change tells us something significant about Americans, according to Paul Blumberg, sociologist at Queens College, New York City.

> They [these trends] demonstrate, I think, a certain confusion about American values these days. Recently, people have looked [for example] not to the top of society for guides to behavior and dress, but to the bottom of the antiestablishment values. Harris Polls taken over the last 10 years show falling public confidence in the leadership of government, large companies, labor, organized religion, and so on, reflecting the social turmoil the country has passed through since about 1960.[14]

Emphasizing his main point concerning status symbols in relation to social values, Blumberg concludes,

> . . . Status symbols are not merely frivolous cocktail party conversation pieces, but are sensitive barometers of scarcity and affluence in society, and also reflect changing social values.[15]

Because of the constant mental turmoil and growing uncertainty that accompany these changes, people begin to feel anxious simply because they do not "belong" if they can't keep up with the trend; they are "different" if they don't meet the ever-fluctuating demands of their surroundings. Suddenly it seems less important to hold onto accepted codes. Honesty is no longer a dominant value; love, no longer a guiding principle. Now all efforts are being directed toward total adjustment to majority opinions as if each person has a built-in radar system attuned to national change. A person "zeroes in" on whatever is dictated or seems desirable to the group, and old values are gradually dropped and exchanged for increased anxiety.

The result?

Culture begins to crumble, and a feverishly cherished permissive liberalization is ironically mistaken for progress.

Perhaps it is progress—but a progress that leads to destruction.

There is probably no system of thought that has entrenched itself so thoroughly in human thinking as evolution—the developmental theory so fiercely advocated by the late Charles Darwin and still defended by his followers. Yet, while there is considerable debate over the evolutionary process with respect to the *individual,* there is very little disagreement over evolutionistic theories with respect to *civilizations.* A common mistake made by Christians who staunchly reject an evolutionary theory in biology is unwittingly to apply an evolutionary perspective to the development of civilizations. Such a perspective places modern Western civilization at the apex of a presumed line of progressive advancement of civilizations—from "primitive" civilizations to modern technological cultures, typical of the Western world.

Lately, however, this theory is seriously being questioned. Recent analysis of ancient civilizations has revealed tremendous achievements yet to be duplicated by the advanced Western world. Many of these have been documented.[16]

Our view of past civilizations has been extremely narrow, and many outstanding advancements of these cultures have been completely ignored. Moreover, historical analysis reveals the progressive decline and fall of *particular* civilizations, but not the progressive advancement of *civilization* per se. The form of various ancient cultures varies with the level of technological achievement, but the basic processes and functions of civilizations apparently have not changed since mankind began gathering into communities.

A notable aspect of Toynbee's monumental *Study of History* is his attempt to deal with two basic facts: (1) that civilizations come into existence, then progress, decline, and finally fall, and (2) that a civilization is itself a single nation.[17] As he began his work (in the first quarter of the twentieth century), Toynbee still looked upon Western civilization as a society that was not as yet *distinctively* declining. But changes have occurred rapidly since then, and we are now confronted with a declining society.

A distinguishing characteristic of the modern world is the use of scientific categories of description and explanation. While our ancestors strove to explain phenomena in terms of Divine Will, modern-day authorities assure us that phenomena are to be looked at only in terms of universal physical processes. These authorities—psychologists, sociologists, and historians—all claim to work according to the "scientific method." True, the social sciences can indeed apply the scientific method in attempting to explain activities involving people; but the scientific method cannot explain all human phenomena, for man is not a solely physical being. Scientific laws can be misapplied and may be short-sighted due to a failure on the part of scientists to recognize their limitations.

To Christians, the Bible remains the source of wisdom for even the most "modern" of issues. What many regard as a unique problem today is just an old issue cloaked in a new disguise— already raised in the Bible centuries ago. Such is the case with the concept of law.

Perhaps the best example of the use of "law" in the Bible lies in the return of Moses from Mount Sinai carrying in his arms the

Ten Commandments carved in two tablets of stone by the fiery finger of God. Moses distinctly described these commandments as from God and part of His *law.* The introduction to the Ten Commandments says, "And God spoke all these words" (Exodus 20:1). The conceptual logic embodied in the Ten Command- ments shows the correct application of the use of the concept "law." For example, they are phrased in the *negative,* with the exception of the fourth, which deals with a commemorative event. God does not tell humanity what to do, but what *not* to do. He requires avoiding specific actions and desires. "Thou shalt *not*" is God's specific command to mankind. All people are cap- able of doing the things prohibited in the Commandments. That a man *can* covet his neighbor's wife is the reason why God prohibits such an act; that a person *can* worship false gods is why God forbids it. The laws of God place limits on personal freedom—for humanity's good.

These "laws of God" apply primarily to humanity in the *moral* sense. God says to mankind, "You *can* worship false gods, but if you do, you violate my prohibition and cannot enter the king- dom of heaven. However, if you *freely* submit yourself to My will, you will live forever in the kingdom of heaven."

It is freedom of action that counts where mankind is con- cerned. The laws of physics, however, do not entail this choice. When a rock falls at the speed of thirty-two feet per second, it falls according to the "law of gravity," a universal law, estab- lished by God and discovered and described by mankind. The rock must fall at this rate since it has only material properties. Error occurs when social scientists attempt to apply similar laws to human behavior. There simply is no mechanistic "law" that governs human behavior. None ever has been or can be dis- covered. Scientists are impotent when trying to use a purely scientific approach to explain human existence and behavior.

The dilemma centers totally in a misapplication of the concept of law. God's laws for mankind allow freedom of choice; those established for everything else do not. The only absolute in the laws for man is that his actions, individually and collectively expressed in history, are subject to the final judgment of God. In examining history, we must assess the development and subsequent fall of civilizations in terms of the proper concept of law—a concept rooted in biblical sources and in God's creation of mankind as free beings.

Historians seek to find "iron laws of history" that account for events the way the law of gravity does in physics. However, it is not surprising that laws have not as yet been discovered, for civilizations represent the collective action of free persons acting in and through time on the very basis of their freedom. Because of this, an analysis of the rise and fall of civilizations must take into account this freedom and place it in the context of God's laws for mankind. History must be assessed in terms of what mankind has done in light of revelations from God. Only by examining history in this context can we hope to discover what truly accounts for the doom of civilizations. Only a "spiritual" approach to history can give a meaningful answer.

History is the record of what mankind has accomplished with the circumstances with which it has been presented. Furthermore, mankind's response to these circumstances will provide criteria for discovering the reasons for the ascent and decline of great civilizations. No other approach can be employed effectively. Modern scientific explanations of distinctively human phenomena encounter difficulty, for they can neither acknowledge nor justify the unique role of the spiritual in human events. Instead, two rather clumsy explanations have been offered. One is the claim that "great men make history," the other that "history makes great men." Neither is worth considering.

Toynbee, in assessing the issue, has given us a choice of two classifications with which to explain national greatness. One is race, the other environment, with both having flaws that are seemingly insurmountable. The racial theory asserts that great civilizations arise because a few select people, uniquely adept and qualified, choose to lead them; the environmental theory states

that a civilization can become great if spawned in favorable surroundings and conditions. The adherents of these theories do not
consider that even though the Jews were God's chosen nation
and certainly had all the qualifications necessary for achieving
national greatness, they never attained it; even Solomon's kingdom pales beside gentile empires before and after. In fact, "great"
nations of history usually did not have godly people as their
leaders.

The plea for "chosen people" is sometimes made in a rather
new and perverted form, that of secular scientism. As Toynbee
pointed out, such theories often use mere physical characteristics
as indicators of superiority.[18] Hitler's Third Reich claimed
superiority for Nietzsche's "blond beast," the Nordic race, scientifically identified by the pompous phrase *homo leucoder-
maticus*. The cruel twist of history shows how misguided "great
men" theories can be, since the two major efforts to apply great
men or chosen people theories to civilizations occur with Jews,
who failed to establish a civilization, and Hitler, whose attempts
to build an empire were quickly extinguished.

The second possibility, the environmental theory, is also
grossly inadequate. For instance, the argument that certain
environmental conditions favor the rise of great civilizations is
weak because many flourished for only a short time, such as
Polynesia, while other civilizations that have arisen in adverse
environmental surroundings have survived longer, such as Egypt.

Both theories contain insufficient substance to qualify as even
a partial answer. It appears that Toynbee may be closer to the
truth than anyone when he points out that in the specific effort
to account for "rise-and-fall," *these two theories apply the proce-
dures of sciences which deal with material things to a problem that is
really spiritual.*[19] Spiritual factors must be considered when attempting to isolate the reasons for the development and demise
of great civilizations. What are these factors, and how do they
interact?

The importance of biblical and spiritual understanding of

human phenomena should not be underestimated. If modern scientific theories fall short of complete explanation, it is because they lack a confrontation with the spiritual dimensions of human potential. But the Bible, with the exception of the major prophetic books, says little about the rise and fall of civilizations. Some of the greatest civilizations were established before biblical times; others emerged after biblical revelation ceased. This silence in Scripture is due to the secular being secondary to the spiritual, in line with Christ's teaching of "render unto Caesar what is Caesar's." But the secular is never to *replace* the spiritual. In a passionate plea which shocked both Russia and the complacent elements in the United States, Alexandr Solzhenitsyn recently "demanded" a return to true spirituality as the only solution to our present dilemma. He said,

> External, or social, freedom is very desirable for the sake of undistorted growth, but it is no more than a condition, a medium, and to regard it as the object of our existence is nonsense. We can firmly assert our inner freedom even in the external conditions of unfreedom. . . . In an unfree environment we do not lose the possibility of progress toward moral goals. The need to struggle against our surroundings rewards our efforts with greater success.[20]

Spirituality has always been closely tied to the history of mankind. It is clear that there would be no history if mankind had not been expelled from the Garden of Eden for violating moral-spiritual laws. History is the record of humanity's struggle for survival necessitated by original sin.

It is clear therefore that from the Fall onward, man's life on this earth cannot progress to the level of Adamic man. Redemption is not to be sought in material forms and hence cannot occur in merely human terms. Thus history becomes a record of man's imperfect existence, rooted in his very own Fall. The Bible reminds us in Genesis that mankind will suffer severely *within* history: "By the sweat of your brow you will eat your food until you return to the ground" (Genesis 3:19). Adverse conditions confront mankind in the world, and man builds his civilizations while struggling against these conditions.

The historical record may be cloudy in some respects, but it is clear on one point: *civilizations cannot emerge without adversity.* The ancient Minoan society, for example, arose partially in challenge to the forests. Similarly the Egyptian, Indian, and Sumerian societies arose in response to decimated lands, while the hard conditions of the Yellow River valley helped lead to the creation of the Shang society. God's plan for mankind acknowledges that it is only in a collective response to adverse conditions that spiritual greatness can be achieved. Is not the Old Testament a record of the trials of the Hebrews as God's chosen people? Did not the prophets undergo great hardships, yet heed the call of their Lord, and was not this the measure of their greatness?

Similarly, the Fall assures that hardships shall follow mankind throughout history. The conquest of environment itself is no guarantee of happiness, for adversity from internal sources is sure to follow.

Mankind's spiritual greatness in history will forever be related to its response to trials and adversity.

Chapter Three

God Moves in History

Accepting the fact that overcoming adversity is a major criterion for the emergence of a civilization, we are forced to deal with two important mechanisms. On the one hand are individuals who, with the help of God, became great leaders because of their success in adversity and who in turn show others the way to follow. On the other hand are "followers" who lack the ability to heed the call directly and passively model their behavior after their leaders, accepting their words and messages without challenge and without conviction. This becomes a simple model for the emergence of great civilizations: (1) leaders who heed the spiritual call in the face of adversity; and (2) citizens who respond to the call by following their chosen leaders.

Only when both leaders and citizens are truly concerned with spiritual matters can greatness be achieved. *A continual spiritual response to mankind's fallen condition is the only valid criterion by which a Christian can evaluate great civilizations.* Technological achievement or military conquest can never be used as a criterion for judging national greatness. This is one of mankind's most dangerous illusions. Such criteria are more appropriately applied to the decline of civilizations than to their ascendancy into greatness.

In recent years, research has shown that many more civilizations must have existed in the distant past than we at first believed. There has been a steadily increasing number of historical and archaeological discoveries at various sites around the world which, because of their mysterious and highly controversial nature, have been classified as "ooparts"—out-of-place artifacts. They are so designated because they are found in geological strata where they shouldn't be, and their sudden appearance in these layers of ancient dirt has puzzled many a trained scientific observer. They emerge from among the remains of the treasured past without evidence of any preceding period of cultural or technological growth. In many cases, the technical sophistication of the ooparts extends far beyond the inventive capabilities of the ancient people we know. The question is, Where do they come from? What civilization(s) do they represent? There is simply no time-slot to accommodate them. Is it possible that the muted voice of the unknown past is trying to get through to us? Is it possible that these ooparts bear testimony to the existence of super-civilizations and developments at a far distant point in human history?

In discussing ancient civilizations that attained both technological and cultural greatness, historians usually begin with Egypt and then continue up the line to the present. However, even our eminent historians have so far failed to find a starting date for the Egyptian civilization. What is its origin?

E. A. Wallis Budge writes in *The Book of the Dead: Papyrus of Ani:*

> The evidence derived from the enormous mass of new material which we owe to the all-important discoveries of the mastabah tombs and pyramids by M. Maspero, and to his publication of the early religious texts, proves beyond all doubt that all the essential texts comprised in the *Book of the Dead,* are, in one form or another, far older than the period of Mena, the first historical king of Egypt. Certain sections, indeed, appear to belong to the predynastic period.
>
> The earliest texts bear within themselves proof not only of having been composed, but also of having been revised, or edited, long before the copies known to us were made, and judging from many passages in the copies inscribed . . . it would seem that even at that remote date (3166 B.C.), the scribes were perplexed and hardly understood the texts which they had before them.[1]

Can you imagine the scribes copying funeral texts left to them from a historical period that in their day was already a nebulous recollection?

What *was* this mysterious source?

There is one possible explanation for the existence of these "remnants" of former cultures, and that is the Genesis story of the Deluge—a flood that is reported to have obliterated all but one family of mankind from the earth in a disaster so destructive, so complete, that one shudders attempting to imagine its totality.

According to the Genesis account, the first race of men, the antediluvian civilization, was highly knowledgeable, being the first to develop agriculture, animal husbandry, construction, political organization, metal working, musical instrumentation, and much more. Genesis tells us that there were ten generations of antediluvians, and among them they developed the basic elements of civilization. Orthodox historians often disregard the significance of the historical books of the Old Testament and with them the story of the Flood and the antediluvian civilization—yet the evidence that they *did* exist and were destroyed in a universal Flood is overwhelming. Approximately 80,000 books pertaining to the Deluge have been written in more than seventy-two languages. Johannes Riem comments in his impressive work, *Die Sintflut in Sage und Wissenschaft*, "Among all traditions there is none so general, so widespread on earth and so apt to show what may develop of the same material according to the varying spiritual character of a people as the Flood traditions."[2] He is referring to more than eighty legends, found among nations circling the globe, that are all concerned with the universal destruction of a once-civilized race. His position is echoed by many other researchers. The noted nineteenth-century Scotsman, Hugh Miller, a geologist and ardent collector of the world's most haunting traditions, writes,

> There is, however, one special tradition which seems to be more deeply impressed and more widely spread than any of the others. The destruction of well-nigh the whole human race, in an early age of the world's history, by a great deluge, appears to have impressed the minds of the survivors, and seems to have been handed down to their children, in consequency, with such terror-struck impressiveness that their remote descendants of the present day have not even yet forgotten it. It appears in almost every mythology and lives in the most distant countries and among the most barbarous tribes.[3]

We discover, in the biblical account of the Deluge (in Genesis 6-9) and in the accumulated legends and traditions, a tale of a terrifying disaster, with sudden torrential rains, devastating waterspouts, and the agonizing cries of drowning people and animals piercing the air. Legends speak of horrendous storms, cataclysmic earthquakes, and a terror-driven rush by man and beast to reach the safety of the ark—the escape vessel—only to be dragged under by the relentless force of the onrushing waters.

Outside the great ship, mankind ceased to exist. Flying reptiles, towering dinosaurs, and the enticing beauty of the antediluvian world perished from the face of the earth.

The destruction was complete—and sudden.

Why did it happen?

It is more than coincidence that the answers to this question suggested by legend and traditions agree with the biblical account. Genesis 6:3, 5-7 tells us,

> Then the LORD said, "My Spirit will not contend with man forever. . . ."
>
> The LORD saw how great man's wickedness on the earth had become, and that every inclination of the thoughts of his heart was only evil all the time. The LORD was grieved that he had made man on the earth, and his heart was filled with pain. So the LORD said, "I will wipe mankind, whom I have created, from the face of the earth—men and animals, and creatures that move along the ground, and birds of the air—for I am grieved that I have made them."

It was the wickedness of mankind through successive generations that caused the world's destruction. The Hawaiian legend of Nu-u, the Righteous Man, tells how the god Kane destroyed the world because man had become so wicked; the ancient Babylonian and Chaldean accounts as well as innumerable other traditions repeat a similar theme.

Although the Bible contains many references to the wickedness of the pre-Flood society, there is little description of it. Disobedience to God, fratricide, lying, violence, and wantonness are mentioned in Genesis, but conditions of widespread degradation, vice, and depravity are implied. Now only vague signs remain of this once vital society. Occasionally the probing spade of archaeology uncovers artifacts that speak of the influence of a race predating the oldest Egyptian dynasty, but generally the earth is strangely silent—hiding its greatest tragedy as if in shame.

When we examine ancient civilizations in search of a formula that can account for the rise and decline of great empires, Egypt certainly must offer prominent evidence. Yet it is not without bias that the Christian approaches any analysis of that once-great civilization, for today's Egypt is not the Egypt of the past. What-ever assessment we make, we must consider one simple fact: the history of any civilization prior to Christ's birth is a history pre-paratory to redemption. The real origin of history is the fall of mankind. Expelled from the Garden of Eden, mankind went forth doomed to exist short of perfection until. . . . Whatever the state of mankind's collective existence prior to the appear-ance of God as Christ, it is clearly a fallen one. Because of this and other factors, any civilization prior to Christ must be viewed in light of three fundamental questions:

- How did the civilization arise and maintain itself without having access to the Word of God?
- What phenomena in civilization *prior to Christ* can be viewed as preparatory to the Word of God?
- What factors within the spectrum of religion prior to Christ account for the downfall of pre-Christian civilizations?

These questions must be applied, not only to Egypt, but to lost civilizations as well. Egypt, however, is outstanding because of three important factors: (1) She is decidedly among the earliest of the great civilizations in recorded history; (2) she is among the most highly developed civilizations—if not the highest—in re-corded history, surviving a span of years unequaled by any civili-zation in postdiluvian history; and (3) she assuredly fell from her greatness.

Egypt today is but a name without a true relationship to her great and glorious past. Hence we can look to Egypt as an exam-ple of a pre-Christian society that experienced a phenomenal rise and fall within the province of God's plan, yet *outside* Christ's plan of redemption.

That the Egyptians did not know Christ is a fact of history, but they were aware of the existence of God, and it is to the knowl-edge of God that civilizations must ultimately be oriented and by it ultimately judged.

The earliest Egyptians battled with harsh conditions of geog-raphy. Egyptian life centered on the great river Nile and developed in relation to the yearly overflow of the river. The flooding both fertilized and destroyed the land. Today Egypt remains 95 percent desert. To its "red land," historians and archaeologists owe as much affection as the country's population owes regret. For, while little of Egypt's masses can survive upon her "red land," almost all the records of her past owe to the desert conditions their survival.

But desolate as the desert was, God was there. Egypt recognized this briefly when, during the eighteenth dynasty, she rose for a fleeting moment to the awareness of monotheism that became one of her greatest legacies. That she fell, embracing polytheism once again, is a sad epitaph.

During her years as an empire, Egypt was not aware of Christ, for He had not as yet arrived in history. However, the fact that Egypt was enlightened as to the power and existence of a single all-powerful god, even prior to the first inscriptions of biblical revelation, is evident.

The emergence of Egypt really begins with her early dynasties. In predynastic Egypt, a collective existence was forged in response to the harsh conditions of the Nile delta. But a mere collective existence is not what is meant by "civilization." Yet the precise reasons for Egypt's emergence into civilization can never be definitely answered. John Wilson comments in his book *The Culture of Ancient Egypt,*

> . . . The final mystery remains: What inner forces lifted the Egyptian toward a new life? Is the entire explanation visible before our eyes in the "urban revolution" and the Mesopotamian catalyst? Or is there still an unknown factor, which is the presence or absence of a spiritual urge toward a new way of life?[4]

A close analysis of Egypt in her early days of imperial glory reveals a culture well beyond total control by nature. It grasped falteringly toward the gods, and eventually toward Yahweh. Even though the rise of Egypt coincides with the development of a complex system of false gods, we owe to this same idolatrous

Egypt an early glimmering awareness of a sovereign god.

Historians concur that by 3100 B.C., after coming to terms with the Nile, Egypt emerged as a great civilization and remained so for nine hundred years. Whether by myth or fact, Menes is credited with uniting the separate and desolate regions around the Nile and "creating" Egypt by joining the land of the Upper and Lower Nile, thereby forming one people, one land, and one citizenry. This outstanding achievement clearly helped Egypt to divert from its pendulous path onto a road marked for greatness, for it was the kind of *spiritual* response to adverse conditions that, as we have stated, signifies the rise of a civilization to prominence.

Exactly why Menes fought for unification no one knows, but it is highly plausible that the yet unrevealed hand of God was already operating in those pre-biblical times. While the revelation of God was not demonstrated at this time in history as it would be to the Hebrews later, an awareness of Him *was* evident in the conditions under which this civilization emerged as a crucible preparing mankind for the birth of the God-man Jesus.

Toynbee has reminded us that technological sophistication per se is not in itself a criterion of greatness. What made Egypt's technological achievements so impressive, both then and now, was its motivation, instigated and embedded in a religious orientation. Rawlinson tells us that even our earliest historian, Herodotus, commented that "the Egyptians are religious to excess, far beyond any other race of men,"[5] and it is precisely this "excessive" religiosity of the Egyptians that accounts for their rise to greatness.

That the unity of the "two lands" could be maintained for so long is a remarkable testimony to the *spiritual* unification of diverse peoples and geographies. The two sections of Egypt were truly one for a long time, banding together spiritually to suggest one god, a single god of all mankind, not merely a god-king or a king of many gods. But this did not occur until Egypt had tasted the bitter fruit of failure and internal illness. For as surely as she prospered during the early dynasties, she fell from spirituality and greatness after the sixth dynasty had passed. Her soul became diseased. Her body politic showed the symptoms of inevitable illness and internal decay. And she lost her enviable place as a spiritual giant among nations.

Looking in retrospect at the demise of Egypt, we find what may be termed the "Decalogue of Egypt's Decay"—ten major characteristics of the dissolution of a once-proud nation:

1. *Success itself became one of Egypt's first failures.* After conquering the adversity of the Nile valley, Egypt softened. Instead of life being focused on a problem common to the whole community, the Egyptian's existence now became easy and complacent. The forces of labor polarized with the upper class exploiting the weaker. This in turn divided the country, and the former unification under which each person worked for the common god-king began to disappear. Individual greed prevailed.

2. *Agnosticism and atheism slowly gained the upper hand.* Egypt had always been a land of many gods and one god-king. Now, with various cities and persons lusting for power and the rule of force, each group of "priests" tried to elevate its own local god to become Egypt's all-powerful god. But these divisions and debates caused Egyptians to begin to lose faith in a single god-king. Various political factions sided with different gods and god-kings, and the unified faith was weakened. Agnosticism and atheism gradually took over, and what little faith remained was often misdirected.

3. *Hedonism began to replace a faithfully guided pragmatism.* The loss of faith combined with the differential push for power led to a society that focused on purely hedonistic activities. Morals and manners declined. Now, instead of maintaining a society held together by mutually shared shames and guilts, the Egyptians pursued anything that "felt good." Work was no longer required of each citizen, and a self-indulgent lifestyle became normal.

4. *Pessimism and cynicism increased.* The lack of a strong moral code rooted in a single god-form led to a cynical and pessimistic

attitude toward society and its citizenry. Temples and tombs were looted. Obedience to the god-king became discretionary according to the prevailing "cynical" political attitude. Careerism and self-interest replaced the serving of others, infiltrating and dominating even the priesthoods.

5. *Decentralization and disintegration increased.* As various groups within Egypt fought for power and control of the state, contending cities began to argue for their right to be the seat of rule for Egypt. Power became decentralized from a single source, the god-king, and drifted to various contending factions. This decentralization led to diverse groups legitimizing their own lifestyles, and Egypt could no longer be considered a unified land comprising the Upper and Lower regions.

6. *Physical might replaced moral force as the source of authority.* No longer was the god-king able to rule by his moral power as god on earth. Now the prevailing rule was based on physical power and might. Force became the "god," and those who were able to wield the strongest destructive power were fated to win. This was the time when great edifices were built with slave-labor. As the ultimate irony, this great civilization enslaved God's own chosen people to work on their pyramids—structures which had degenerated from glorious tombs of the kings into personal monuments of lesser political leaders. No wonder the workmanship and artistic details found in the later pyramids are universally recognized as considerably inferior to the great pyramids of the earlier dynasties!

7. *Secularism and materialism emerged and increased.* The "scientific attitude" in Egypt after the Old Kingdom became increasingly influential. No longer were science and materialism restrained by a basically spiritual approach that subordinated technology to morality; rather a new "technological morality" emerged in which theological concerns took second place to what was scientifically and technologically feasible.

8. *Resistance to foreign influences and domination weakened.* Her developing internal weakness left Egypt prey to foreign forces as

never before in her history. This protected land, allowed to develop internally for almost a thousand years in the Old Kingdom, was now susceptible to conquest by foreign armies. Eventually Egypt could no longer withstand the attacks of the Hyksos and submitted to their brutal rule, initiating a period in Egyptian history that John A. Wilson has aptly termed "the Great Humiliation."

9. *Confusion and alienation came to dominate the lower classes.* Confronted by various power groups demanding allegiance, the average Egyptian became confused and alienated from his own culture. Not only was he unsure of his beliefs, but his allegiance was dissipated. Who was to be followed? Who was right? Who was wrong? His entire way of life and thinking became disoriented, and the disintegration of Egyptian culture was reflected in miniature in the disintegration of the average Egyptian's life. It became obvious that the national strength of Egypt could no longer be derived from the strength of its individual citizens.

10. *A hypocritical priesthood began to run the country.* As factions and cities vied for political power in a disintegrating Egypt, various priesthoods defended their local gods in hopes of sharing the spoils of power. The religious leaders of the country became vulgarized, and religion itself became antithetical to spirituality. Rather than guiding the nation, religious leaders became followers and patrons of petty political whims and maneuvered feverishly for power and political protection. Thus the final tear appeared in the moral fabric of a once-proud nation.

From the seventh through seventeenth dynasties (c. 2200-c. 1550 B.C.), Egypt still appeared to be something of a single land, loosely united yet, in comparison with the Old Kingdom, really a mere shell of her former greatness. The schism in her soul was deep. Humanly speaking, there was no hope left. That she did not falter totally at that time is due to other forces—forces that make this the finest chapter in Egypt's history.

At the nadir of her demise, Egypt tried to rise again under the rule of a child-king. Under this ruler, Akhnaton, she came near to surrendering the worship of many false deities to the worship of the one true God.

It is God's prerogative to work through whom He chooses. Yet is it not also true that He manifests to others a glimpse of His reality, however incomplete the view? Akhnaton was not a prophet of God, for God's prophets were of the Hebrew race. Yet no gentile to that time came so near to expressing truths so similar to those revealed by God to His chosen people.

Who was this man Akhnaton, and how did he emerge from a disintegrated Egyptian society?

Today in Central Park in New York City, an obelisk of imposing dimensions stands tall and impressive above the heads of those who pause to gaze at it. It is the obelisk of Thutmose III, the great-grandfather of the ruler Egypt would come to know as Akhnaton. On the obelisk are inscribed these words: "The smiter of the rulers of foreign countries who had attacked him."

Thutmose III was a warrior who ruled at least one hundred years after the conquering Hyksos had finally been driven from Egypt. Explusion of these invaders in the eighteenth dynasty ushered in the New Empire about 1550 B.C. Thutmose III conducted many campaigns in Syria and raised Egypt to her highest height militarily—a striking contrast to his descendant, Akhnaton, who years later would renounce military force, let the territorial gains crumble away, and promote worship of one god above all gods as the only true power.

The succeeding kings Thutmose IV and Amenophis upheld the warrior tradition. But Amenophis's son, Amenhotep, who married Nefertiti and ascended the throne at the youthful age of thirteen, changed the course of the empire and Egypt's cultural and religious life in a series of radical reforms that provide for him a lasting place in history.

Amenhotep's mother, Queen Tiy, initially exercised much control in the rule of the nation. But in the third or fourth year of his brief reign, Amenhotep claimed the title "Pharaoh," a term formerly reserved for the place in which the king resided, and took the name "Akhnaton," a name imbued with unmistakable religious importance. It signified the desire of the young ruler to promote the worship of one god, Aton, and rebuke the pantheon of deities that had long characterized Egyptian religion.

Akhnaton constructed a city, Karnak, dedicated to the one god and called it "the City of the Horizon." At the age of twenty-one he moved to the city and proclaimed the worship of Aton as the official religion of the empire. He demanded that all other gods' names be effaced from public buildings and commemorative plaques.

In keeping with this monotheistic spirit, temple artisans were encouraged to be more realistic in their reliefs depicting the Pharaoh, and not idealistic as preceding rulers had required. This change reflected Akhnaton's view of subservience to a higher power and renunciation of the concept of earthly rule by a god-king. Recognizing that he ruled in the name of a god and not *as* a god was a humble admission of his humanness.

Furthermore, Akhnaton's plea for monotheism was a return to the first great spiritualization of Egypt expressed however ineffectively in the Old Kingdom. Akhnaton regarded polytheism as but a crude form of religion. It is to the spiritual Egypt, initiated in the Old Kingdom and elevated to glorious heights by Akhnaton, that we look for the true marks of her greatness. Egypt had searched for a "First Unifying Principle" two thousand years *before* the Greeks or the Hebrews; but with Akhnaton, the First Unifying Principle as one god above all gods was established.

Yet history moves on relentlessly, and a swift seventeen years after it began, Egypt's flirtation with monotheism was over, undoubtedly representing one of the greatest "missed moments" of history. *If* Akhnaton's monotheism had survived, what might have been the future of Egypt? How differently would God have treated her? Ironically Egypt, the first antediluvian civilization to express monotheism was also the one to wield the whip of persecution on God's chosen people.

Akhnaton and the Egypt of the eighteenth dynasty were

definitely "pre-Christian," but still far from being truly
"Christian." Whether God chose Egypt to lead, we do not know,
but we do get the distinct feeling that Egypt under Akhnaton
reached out for God and rose to a glimpse of His glory. Weigall
writes,

> By no religion in the world is Christianity so closely approached
> as by the faith of Akhnaton; and if the Pharao's doctrines as to
> immortality are not altogether convincing, neither are the
> Christian doctrines, as they are now interpreted, altogether with-
> out fault. In the above pages, it has been necessary to compare
> Akhenaton's creed with Christianity, since there is so much
> common between the two religions; but it should be remembered
> that this comparison must of necessity be unfavorable to the
> Pharao's doctrine, revealing as it does its shortcomings. Let the
> reader remember that Akhenaton lived some thirteen hundred
> years before the birth of Christ, at an age when the world was
> steeped in superstition and sunk in the fogs of idolatry. Bearing
> this in mind, he will not fail to see in that tenderly loving Father
> whom the boy-Pharaoh worshipped an early revelation of the God
> to whom we of the present day bow down; and once more he will
> find how true are the words—"God fulfills Himself in many
> ways."[6]

After Akhnaton, Egypt, though weakened, survived as a major
power through her twentieth dynasty (until about 100 B.C.),
when she was once again conquered, never again rising to her
former power.

The remainder of Egypt's history is one of decay, disintegration, and spiritual death as was the case after the Old Kingdom—but this time the disease was fatal!

To the Christian, the fact that Egypt became the enslaver of
the Hebrews is perhaps the ultimate irony. History indicates that
Pharaoh Ramses II, father of more than five hundred children,
was the dreaded Pharaoh of the Exodus, but there are very few
references to the Hebrews in any text discovered thus far.
Perhaps the only exception is the poetical inscription celebrating
Egypt's military might and victories under Ramses II.

> The princes are prostrate, saying "Mercy!"
> Not one raises his head among the Nine Bows;
> Desolation is for Tehunu; Hatti is pacified;
> Plundered is the Canaan with every evil;
> Carried off is Ascalon; seized upon is Gezer;
> Yonoam is made as that which does not exist;
> Israel is laid waste, his seed is not;
> Palestine is become a widow of Egypt;
> All lands together, they are pacified.
> Everyone who was restless has been bound
>   by Mer-ne-Prah.[7]

This is indeed a minute reference to a great moment in history—one that is easily lost among the shifting years of time. Yet it is the only one known that refers to Egypt's struggle with a conquered foe. Perhaps it would have been different had Egypt taken up the challenge to accept the true God in the time of Akhnaton.

But Egypt did not, and Israel too failed to remain true.

History has recorded their sad demise, for apart from God no nation remains strong.

Chapter Four

Destruction of a Golden Empire

World history is in reality merely a chronicle of man's inability to direct his own affairs, and there appears to have been no exceptions.

Throughout the centuries after the demise of Egypt, civilizations continued to reject divine guidance, yet God persevered in giving His counsel. The events surrounding the biblical prophet Daniel show this in a most decisive way.

Daniel's prophetic ability probably never would have gained such great renown had it not been for Nebuchadnezzar's siezure of Jerusalem in 606 B.C., and the resulting transport of the conquered Hebrews to the land of Babylon. Consistent with the ancient customs governing the spoils of war, a number of young Israelite nobles—among them Daniel—were in the wailing throngs who trudged through the desert sands into Babylonian captivity to begin a new existence as slaves among the Princes of the East.

For seventy long years, from 606 to 536 B.C., Daniel resided at the court of Babylon—first as a captive nobleman, later as a court official—spending most of his time as prime minister of the monarchy, directing the Babylonian affairs of state at the pinnacle of its greatness. Uriah Smith says of Daniel, "From the height of its glory he saw that kingdom decline, and pass into other hands. Its period of greatest prosperity was embraced within the limits of the lifetime of one man."[1]

Prosperity, glory, and fame are appropriate terms to describe the land of Nebuchadnezzar. It was founded by Nimrod, the great-grandson of Noah, more than two thousand years before Christ. "Cush was the father of Nimrod, who grew to be a mighty one on the earth," we are told in Genesis 10:8-10. "He was a mighty hunter before the LORD; that is why it is said, 'Like Nimrod, a mighty hunter before the LORD.' The first centers of his kingdom were Babylon, Erech, and Akkad and Calneh, in Shinar."

It must have been an unbelievable sight to the travel-worn Hebrews as they entered the portals of Babylon for the first time, for it was a metropolis unsurpassed in beauty. Situated on the Euphrates, it had continued to grow steadily from a primitive settlement of fishing huts along the sandy banks of a swamp to an immense city encircled by impregnable walls.

Built to withstand the onslaught of the mightest armies of its day, Babylon's defenses were the work of architectural geniuses. The walls enclosed the city in a double line of fortifications, with the outer walls approximately fifty feet high and ten feet wide. In addition to the outer wall, the engineers had constructed an even thicker line of defense, consisting of a twenty-five-foot-wide mustering ground, plus an inner wall of twenty feet, making a defense line fifty-five feet wide altogether. And all along this huge wall were watchtowers spaced about one hundred yards apart. The total length of the fortified wall surrounding the city was just under ten miles. Impressive indeed—but there was one weak spot.

James Wellard says in *Babylon,*

> The principal problem in the defense of Babylon was the passage of the Euphrates right through the middle of the city, the old part of which lay on the east bank, the new on the west bank. Herodotus mentions this fact, noting that the river was broad, deep and swift and that the city wall was extended some way downstream and then brought back on both sides to the edge of the banks. The weak point in the system was, of course, the possibility of an army of enemy boats slipping past the river forts at night and so penetrating the very heart of the city. Nebuchadnezzar attempted to correct this weakness by building immense forts to the north of the city . . . and by diverting the water of the Euphrates via a canal into the great moat which followed the line of the city walls.
>
> Inside the defense system the political life of the capital centered on the palace which Nebuchadnezzar made the most magnificent royal residence of the world, while the equally important religious activities of this theocratic state were directed from the temple of the god Marduk.[2]

The Chaldean or Second Babylonian Empire succeeded the Assyrian. Its culture and many of its people were descended from the Babylonians of old, but its ruling classes were Chaldeans whose Aramean ancestors had invaded Babylonia centuries earlier. Under Nebuchadnezzar, one of their descendants, the Chaldean Empire celebrated its Golden Age. His abilities as a cunning statesman and military commander are so highly regarded by scholars that they need no elaboration here. His contemporary, the prophet Jeremiah, recognized very early in Nebuchadnezzar's reign that he was the new power in international politics and prophesied that his empire would endure for three generations (Jeremiah 27:7). Not only did Nebuchadnezzar excel in military matters, but he created a cultural unity throughout the land that was unequaled.

There was no empire like this. Yet he himself was a captive of gross superstition, fearful to move without the explicit permission of the gods, i.e., until he found the true God toward the end of his life. Superstition lay at the heart of Babylonian religion, with astrology and necromancy giving it its most characteristic expression. H. W. F. Saggs writes of the religion,

> Although the decisions of the gods were arbitrary, mankind was not left without indications of the divine will. The intentions of the gods were supposed to be reflected or foreshadowed in events on earth, even the most trivial. The Babylonians saw the universe as a whole, and believed that what happened in one part was mirrored in another.[3]

Hence, the Babylonians' great reliance on astrology.

Babylon was definitely an empire based on superstition and brute military force, yet within it were weaknesses that can only be recognized in retrospect. The collapse of Assyrian rule between 625 and 612 B.C. did not bring all government to ruin in the Mesopotamian region; otherwise, it would not have been possible for the successor-state, Babylonia, to reach its Golden Age within thirty years after. The shift to Babylonian administration produced changes that gave the provincial governors a freer hand and left less power in the hands of the king. The domestic history of Babylonia during the time of the prophet Daniel became in many aspects a struggle for power between the dynasty and the temple corporations.

The average Babylonian citizen, however, was not aware of the struggle. To him, living in the Golden Age under Nebuchadnezzar was the ultimate. At regular intervals, the standing armies of the king would raid the surrounding kingdoms and divide the spoils with the citizens of Babylon. Exquisite beauty encompassed them on all sides, and the grandeur of the Babylonian architecture became the pride of all inhabitants. But most important of all treasures was the assurance to the Babylonian citizenry that their lives were protected by the laws of Hammurabi, the legacy of the greatest king of the Amorite dynasty of Babylon. Hammurabi (c. 1800 B.C.) instituted a code of laws equal in many ways to the laws of Moses given to the children of Israel during their sojourn in the desert some three hundred years later.

This Code of Hammurabi, now preserved in the British Museum, is the most complete and refined expression of Babylonian law. It is obvious from its composition that the code was to be applied to a much wider realm than any single country. Despite the inscriptions relating to family solidarity, district responsibility, trial by ordeal, and the law of retaliation, the code went far beyond tribal custom and recognized no blood feud, private retribution, or marriage by capture. No nation lived as securely protected by law as the Babylonians.[4] Under the shelter of the code, the Babylonians enjoyed free citizenship, private landownership, free medical care provided by the employer, controlled commercial transactions, and compulsory service in the armed forces and public works corps. There were also regulations requiring farmers to cultivate a minimum area of their tillable land, providing for government-controlled irrigation projects, setting wage rates, and providing fixed punishments for code violations.

But there was more. While Babylonian marriages were customarily arranged by the parents, divorce proceedings were strictly controlled with provisions made for the wife and children. Adoption also was governed by law, as were matters of inheritance and monetary compensation for willful injury. Even judges were held responsible for their acts, and those found to be corrupt were permanently removed from office. Not until the Ten Commandments and the law of Moses were introduced to the Hebrews did a more workable set of laws exist anywhere!

Such was the way of life when Daniel entered the city as a captive in 606 B.C. But within seventy years the gold that was Babylon was replaced by the silver of the Medo-Persians. It was under King Nabonidus, a successor to Nebuchadnezzar, that the process of national degeneration politically, economically, and morally set in, resulting in the demise of the empire through neglect and degradation.

Nabonidus seems to have spent his entire seventeen-year reign restoring the temples of his country and tracing its history to the origins of the nations. Accompanied by an impressive retinue of historians, archaeologists, and architects, he traversed his kingdom, giving careful attention to the progress of his nationwide building programs, but left the administration of the realm to his son Belshazzar. Completely indifferent to political, economic, and military matters, Nabonidus wandered on, oblivious to the increasing power of Cyrus of Anshan, a desert tribal king. By the time the stark reality of impending danger to his kingdom finally became apparent to him, Babylonia's trade routes to the north had already been severed. Within a few years

> the balance of power in western Asia was entirely altered. Babylon was no longer secure to north and east; instead she was faced by one single power, young, vigorous and rapidly expanding, backed by all the resources of Asia Minor and Iran. It must have been obvious that the Babylonian empire would be the next objective, but for some unfathomable reason Nabonidus in his desert capital failed to see this.[5]

The fact that Babylon was governed as a theocracy with power to rule descending from the gods did not prevent the nation from splitting into warring factions. While racial feelings may have been one of the underlying factors, controversies between the priests of Marduk and the military and business leaders of the capital finally tore the country apart. Yet Belshazzar, like his father, was unmindful of the trouble besetting his country. Ignoring the developing internal dissent and unwilling or perhaps unable to stop the advances of Cyrus in the northern area, he closed his eyes to the mounting problems and decided to wait. . . . Belshazzar was far from a politician; he was a playboy and felt no responsibility toward affairs of state. The end was rapidly approaching, and it was left to the prophet Daniel to give us the final details of the dying days of the Babylonian Empire (Daniel 5:1-6).

> King Belshazzar gave a great banquet for a thousand of his nobles and drank wine with them. While Belshazzar was drinking his wine, he gave orders to bring in the gold and silver goblets that Nebuchadnezzar his father* had taken from the temple in Jerusalem, so that the king and his nobles, his wives and his concubines might drink from them. So they brought in the gold goblets that had been taken from the temple of God in Jerusalem, and the king and his nobles, his wives and his concubines drank from them. As they drank the wine, they praised the gods of gold and silver, of bronze, iron, wood and stone.
>
> Suddenly the fingers of a human hand appeared and wrote on the plaster of the wall, near the lampstand in the royal palace. The king watched the hand as it wrote. His face turned pale and he was so frightened that his knees knocked together and his legs gave way.

What was the mysterious message that had appeared so suddenly on the wall? Daniel, as one of the king's wisemen, supplied the interpretation.

Citing the pride of the king, his defiance of the true God, and his blasphemous action in using the vessels of the Jewish temple for his idolatrous feasts, Daniel pronounced judgment on the king as follows (Daniel 5:25-28):

> "This is the inscription that was written:
>> MENE, MENE, TEKEL, PARSIN
> "This is what these words mean:
> *Mene:* God has numbered the days of your reign and brought it to an end.
> *Tekel:* You have been weighed on the scales and found wanting.
> *Peres:* Your kingdom is divided and given to the Medes and Persians."

And while Daniel was still speaking, the Medo-Persians were

---

*Following Babylonian custom, Belshazzar referred to his grandfather as father. The word can be translated "ancestor" or "predecessor."

launching their attack. For a number of years, Cyrus and his vice-regent Darius had been fighting the armies of the Babylonian Empire in various regions, and finally, in the third year of Belshazzar's reign, Cyrus decided to lay siege to Babylon, the only major city in all the East that still resisted them. The Babylonians gathered within their seemingly impregnable walls, with provisions on hand to last some twenty years. The land within the confines of their broad city was sufficient to furnish food for both the inhabitants and the garrison for an indefinite period. They scoffed at Cyrus from their lofty walls and derided his apparently useless efforts to bring them into subjection.

According to all human calculation, the Babylonians had good reason for their assuredness and optimism. Weighed on the scales of earthly probability, the city could never be conquered with the means of warfare then known.

> In their feeling of security lay the source of danger. Cyrus resolved to accomplish by stratagem what he could not effect by force. Learning of the approach of an annual festival in which the whole city would be given up to mirth and revelry, he fixed upon that day as the time to carry his purpose into execution.[6]

What he planned is told us by Herodotus.

> Whether then, someone advised him in his difficulty, or he perceived for himself what to do, I know not, but this he did: he posted his army at the place where the river enters the city, and another part of it where the stream issues from the city, and had his men enter the city by the channel of the Euphrates when they should see it to be fordable.
>
> Having so arrayed them and given his command, he himself marched away with those of his army who could not fight; and when he came to the lake, Cyrus dealt with it and with the river just as had the Babylonian queen: drawing off the river by a canal into the lake, which was till now a marsh, he made the stream to sink till its former channel could be forded. When this happened, the Persians who were posted with this intent made their way into Babylon by the channel of the Euphrates, which had now sunk about to the height of the middle of a man's thigh.[7]

Guided by two Babylonian traitors—Gobyras, the Babylonian governor of Gutium, and Godatas, a man about whom history is silent—the troops made ready for the attack. Yet all this would have been in vain had not the entire city given itself over to a night of unrestrained merriment and presumptuousness, two factors that Cyrus was counting on. Moreover, his fording the river would have been to no avail if the Babylonians had not made one drastic error in their defense plans. On each side of the river throughout the entire length of the city were walls of great height and of equal thickness with the outer walls. In these walls were massive gates of brass which, when closed and guarded, debarred all entrance from the riverbed to any of the streets that crossed the river. Had the gates been closed at this time, the soldiers of Cyrus might have marched to the city along the river bed and marched right out again, for they would not have been able to enter the city. But in the drunken orgy of that night, the guards had neglected to shut the river gates, as Isaiah the prophet had predicted years before when he warned, "This is what the LORD says to his anointed, to Cyrus, whose right hand I take hold of to subdue nations before him and to strip kings of their armor, to open doors before him so that gates will not be shut" (Isaiah 45:1).

The wild feast hosted by Belshazzar cost the Babylonians their kingdom. Uriah Smith writes,

> They went into their brutish revelry subjects of the king of Babylon; they awoke from it slaves to the king of Persia. The soldiers of Cyrus first made known their presence in the city by falling upon the royal guards in the vestibule of the palace of the King. Belshazzar soon became aware of the cause of the disturbance and died, fighting for his life.[8]

Daniel comments briefly in his historical account, "That very night Belshazzar, king of the Babylonians, was slain, and Darius the Mede took the kingdom, at the age of sixty-two" (Daniel 5:30-31).

It was a dramatic and tragic end to a glorious empire, and

history records it as such. A backward glance at the events surrounding and preceding Babylon's fall, however, reveals a long chain of circumstances that were influential in the dissolution of the empire—events that began about the time of Daniel's entry into the city in 606 B.C. True, the mistakes of history are always easy to judge in retrospect, but it is equally obvious that a nation's moral and military fiber does not unravel overnight. In examining the history of the last seventy years of the empire, we find elements contributing to its overthrow that should have served as dire warnings to the Medo-Persians, the Greeks, and the Romans who ruled in years to come—but no matter how plain these signs were, no one took them seriously.

Suggestive of today, some of the problems of Babylon were caused by a controversy concerning state's rights versus temple or religious rights. During the last seven decades of the empire, a powerful struggle ensued between the royal dynasty and the temple "corporations." Disregarding the elementary principles of the governing Code of Hammurabi, the kings had become intoxicated with unlimited power. Flouting the law, they installed special royal officers in the temples for the purpose of taxing the temple corporations.

While Nebuchadnezzar for a short time accepted the God of the Hebrews (see Daniel 4:28-37), his immediate successor Amelmarduk soon returned to heathen worship, living by ungovernable passion until a group of army officers, desiring a return to a semblance of the imperial glory of Nebuchadnezzar's reign, assassinated him.

The Babylonians' rejection of God came simultaneously with actions designed to discredit and destroy the Jewish inhabitants of the city. Throughout the years, the Semitic "immigrants" had become increasingly unpopular with many Babylonians because of favoritism shown them by the government's placing them in ruling positions in the king's palace. The Jews thus held civil service jobs that native Babylonians claimed were theirs. Jealousy and greed began to spread.

Among economic factors, food now became scarce in some areas—a problem the government confronted by granting huge agricultural loans, giving itself the right to determine what was to be grown and where. The situation worsened when thousands who should have worked the fields continued to be employed in building temples and palaces for the king's glorification; and tens of thousands other able-bodied men remained in the monarch's standing army for years at a time, further reducing national productivity. In addition, the marauding armies of Cyrus had been able to cut the customary trade routes, isolating the economy of Babylon to a large extent from that of the surrounding countries. Combined with new trade restrictions established by the government, this rapidly spawned skyrocketing inflation. In the years 560-550 B.C., prices of both commodities and services soared by as much as 200 percent.

Still the empire might have been salvaged had it not been for the desecration of two of the country's most sacred institutions: religion and family. With the religion of Yahweh having been purged from government, heathen institutions once more became the guiding force of the land. Astrology—a specialty of the Babylonians—and idolatry regained prominence. Necromancy and dream interpretation once again displaced reliance on godly inspiration. Evil power and superstition became the "voice of the gods," giving advice for daily living, eroding the remnants of a faith in one true God, and undermining family life that once was governed by law, decency, and divine guidance. Even though Nebuchadnezzar was dead, his memory lingered as did traces of his faith in the God of the Hebrews. Many of the Babylonians probably remembered the royal decree once issued by the king:

King Nebuchadnezzar,
   To the peoples, nations and men of every language, who live in all the world:
   May you prosper greatly!
   It is my pleasure to tell you about the miraculous signs and wonders that the Most High God has performed for me.

> How great are his signs,
>   how mighty his wonders!
> His kingdom is an eternal kingdom;
>   his dominion endures from
>   generation to generation.
>
> (*Daniel 4:1-3*)

It is significant that the woes befell the empire *following* Nebuchadnezzar's death—after the nation had returned to pagan worship.

If society suffered, family life suffered even more. Whereas matters pertaining to family structure were previously governed by Hammurabi's Code, now lawlessness prevailed, and the nation was given over to adultery, divorce, and prostitution. Perverts roamed the streets, and lesbians, homosexuals, and transvestites occupied the halls of government. The empire had truly disintegrated and now lay quivering and vulnerable to the eventual invasion by the Medo-Persian armies. And the internal fifth column, collaborating with the Persians, took care of that. No one knows the exact duration of Cyrus's siege, but in only one night of drunkenness and sexual debauchery, the Babylonian Empire's doom was sealed.

Thus history had added another example to the growing list of nations that tried to thrive without God.

Chapter Five

The Failure
of Reason

The origin of the Greeks, like that of so many other civilizations, is shrouded in mystery. The ancient history of Greece begins somewhere around the second millennium before Christ and is characteristically identified as the "dark ages"— dark, not because they represent a lack of development, but because history reveals so little about them.

Contrary to what is commonly thought, the people we call Greeks today never identified themselves as Greeks in their earliest history. The name "Greek" is derived from the Roman *Graeci*, which is the name the Romans gave these cultured people they conquered. The "Greeks" called their own land

Hellas and probably referred to themselves as the Hellenes. Fiercely proud, they mistrusted all foreigners and despised everyone whose language did not sound like theirs. All indications are that their evaluation of the non-Greek was harsh and total. Even though the Greeks contributed many principles that led to the superiority of Western civilization, they also bore within them the root sin of all humanism: pride.

Who *really* were these people we know as the Greeks?

Ancient history tells us that the Greeks are direct descendants of the mixed-blood peoples known to historians as the Mycenaeans of the Bronze Age. They inhabited the Peloponnese, the southern portion of modern Greece, around 1200 B.C. However, for a four-hundred-year period of their history—1200-800 B.C.—history presents us with an information vacuum, the "dark ages" of which we know only the shadows. Major civilizations appear to have flourished in various parts of the world during that time, but the Peloponnese did not reemerge until 800 B.C., when the use of iron ended the Bronze Age. Iron and Greece rose together, fashioning a future that influenced the globe and created a heritage that forms the backbone of the Western world. Much of the greatness of the United States is a result of this influence, but ironically much of the spiritual blindness of our society today is the same blindness that brought darkness to Greece.

As Toynbee has noted, a simple factor in judging a civilization's possibility for greatness is the response of a people to severe geographical conditions. In the case of Greece, the country's harsh geographical conditions are not immediately evident. Greece has always been ruled by a temperate climate; this may account for the mild temperament of contemporary Greeks. The land itself, however, exhibits a ruthless severity. It is a country governed by mountain peaks, with her islands but the tips of mountains groping up from the sea floor. Between the rugged heights flow gentle, fertile valleys where individual city-states arose with total independence of one another even though geographically they could be considered neighbors. The distance involved in maneuvering around the mountains kept the city-states apart, creating a high degree of self-sufficiency for them.

Because of its mountainous terrain, the land of Greece has never been able to support a large population. True, the mountains containing marble and limestone provided enough raw material for construction and art, but they yielded very little in forage for the flocks, which in turn resulted in a scarce supply of butter. The production of olive oil is but one example of their desperate efforts to supplement their needs. The harsh mountain conditions dictated the emergence of a tough-minded people whose intellectual ability matched the sharp contours of their limited land.

Though totally hemmed in by a maze of mountains, the Greeks could always look out to the vastness of the seas. Because of the immensity of the seas, another characteristic of the Greeks was born: the ability to use their imagination to reach *beyond* the limitations of their natural boundaries. Hence, isolated and protected as they were, the Greeks became unified as one people, fiercely individual, yet speaking a common language, sharing the same heritage, and impelled by an insatiable imagination. For whatever the differences existing between the city-states, the Greeks were no barbarians. They understood the variations in Greek dialects and knew that they were part of one people. They were superior and proud, and their legacy to Western civilization has been one of their crowning achievements.

Yet their legacy was grounded on false gods. The false god of critical Reason and the god of Unlimited Imagination were mere reflections of the fluidity of the vast open seas. They were separate, yet they conspired together to assure that one of the greatest of the great civilizations would bring itself to ruin. Ironically these same gods can be found today in the America of the eighties. The heritage we have gained from Greece contains much to be admired together with a dire warning that reason and imagination alone cannot sustain a civilization no matter how great its temporary achievement.

The limitlessness of the Greek imagination is a matter of historical record. Indeed, the earliest Greek children lived in a world transmitted to them in marvelous stories and tales of adventuresome Greek heroes and heroines. Pandora and her box; Hercules and his feats of strength; the Argonauts and the search for the Golden Fleece; the beauty of Helen and the fall of Troy—such tales are immortal. Yet, to the Greeks these myths—fantastic as they were—served to solidify the city-states into one people and provided a singularly meaningful interpretation of life's events.

As children today learn about Santa Claus, so children in ancient Greece learned their myths. But there is a vast difference between them. The young American child is usually taught that the rotund gentleman called Santa who lives at the North Pole with his elves and reindeer is just a story and not to be taken seriously, especially when one reaches adulthood. For the Greeks, however, the legends and tales were considered truth forever, an ultimate reality base that explained life in an imaginative way. And it is here that we see the hidden hand of God. The mythical tales woven from human imagination were in fact not true, yet they pointed to a reality that cannot be easily understood. A parallel between Greek mythology and biblical events is often drawn as if the Bible itself is just another collection of man's myths. But this is not the position of the believing Christian.

The Greek mind expressed a desire for a purposeful description of life and man's place in that life. But functioning without direct inspiration from God, the Greek mind could grasp only half the truth. The myths and gods of man remained mere imagination, and the individual who uses them for guidance will never rise above the primitive understanding of a child. The stories of the Scripture are God's words, and the person who believes this is a child of God forever.

The mythical tales of the Greeks inspired great works of art, literature, and poetry—all products of the ability of the Greeks to use the imaginative powers inherent in mankind. But man-kind was made for more than just that. The mind allows people to transcend reason and open themselves up to God's word. The ancient Hellenes used their powers to create only what man alone can create, never catching a glimpse of the glory of God.

It has often been said that people get the gods they deserve. In this respect, the Greeks were no exception, for their gods were human—very human. The artistic skill of the ancient Greeks is well recognized; their majestic buildings, realistic statues, and grand memorials all testify to this even in their present ruin. Paradoxically the human figures so aptly represented in stone are hardly differentiated from their marble gods. The statues of the Greek gods obviously have human form. Indeed, only a people with crassly human gods would have depicted a god urinating, as is the case with one famous statue of Hercules. Here in stark realism are defined the limits of the Greek imagination. However expressive the Greeks were in their art, the gods produced by such a creative process remained but sordid external projections of mere humans. No wonder the Greek legends and myths rep-resent their gods as bickering and protesting among themselves and acting even in moments of greatness in the most human way.

Firmly rooted in Greek soil is the "theology" of the oracle and the mystery cults. Even the most rational of the Greek philoso-phers are said to have consulted the oracles and to have heeded their ambiguous advice, an obvious forerunner to the belief in modern-day psychics. Jeane Dixon, for example, has often told the story of her advising President Roosevelt, true or untrue. For the Greeks, the Delphic oracle, linked with the god Apollo, was most famous. While there were many others, the oracle at Del-phi is the most outstanding example of Greek "supernatural guidance." Here a priestess sat near a fissure in Mount Parnassus from which emanated a natural gas. The gas, having the ability to alter normal states of consciousness, left the priestess ranting, often incoherently. A priest stood nearby to "interpret" the ramblings of the drugged priestess to the seekers after "guidance." The real power lay with the priest, for it was he, as a channel of communication, who wielded awesome influence and authority. For instance, it is said that when King Croesus of Lydia sought advice concerning the wisdom of his invasion of Persia from the oracle at Delphi, it gave him an ambiguous and all-too-clever answer.

"If you do," the priest interpreted, "a mighty empire will be overthrown."

Croesus launched the invasion, and history records his defeat. The oracle with its indeterminate counsel was vindicated by his fall. Of course, had Persia succumbed to the might of Croesus, the oracle would also have been correct, but in a more direct fashion.

Thus, the religious establishment surrounding the oracles possessed the persuasive power of ambiguity, and as with the marbled statues of the gods, the Greeks came to mistake mere interpretative sophistry for divine wisdom.

But if the religion of the Greeks was too limited, formed upon projections of mankind's own insufficient nature, the effort to dethrone religion today in the name of the new god of Reason has proved to be just as restricting.

The Greeks are as well known for their rational minds as for their religious superstition. The roll of the Greek philosophers is a "who's who" of philosophy, and it has often been said that all subsequent Western philosophy is nothing more than a footnote to Plato and Aristotle. *The keen and cultivated rational Greek mind is the foundation of the arrogance of modern humanism in which pride is mistaken for worship, and reason has become a substitute for belief in God.*

The Greeks excelled in mathematics. Perhaps many of their achievements were based on extensions of the practical mathematics of the Egyptians; but while the Egyptians used mathematics as a tool to build their pyramids, the Greeks regarded it as a rational exercise in and of itself. Seeing "all things as num-bers" as Pythagoras did, the Greeks not surprisingly became con-cerned with geometry, the mathematics of form. This triumph of the rational mind was mistakenly elevated to a "religion" in which the rational manipulation of numbers was substituted for the "unraveling" of the ultimate mysteries of life. That scientists today pursue quantitative orientations in search of an "absolute truth" is but an extension of the legacy of Greek mathematics. The limitations are all too obvious. The wisdom of God is not to be "discovered" in any formula, however sophisticated.

As with mathematics, so it was with philosophy. The Greeks, uninspired by the true Word of God, questioned the nature and origin of the world and all that is in it. The inadequacy of Greek myths was apparent, and eventually purely rational answers were sought to these puzzling problems. From this pursuit emerged a virtual torrent of literary explanations, of which only fragments and portions survive. These fragments are impressive, for they are subtle, persuasive, and provocative; but for all its achieve-ments, Greek philosophy remained incomplete within itself.

Reason elevated to a god is truly only another of the weaker gods. It *alone* cannot lead to God, nor can it resolve the mystery of the Word of God for those who do not have the faith to understand. As the apostle Paul noted, the crucifixion of Jesus is foolishness to those who have only reason (1 Corinthians 1:23), but for those who by faith exceed reason, the crucifixion is a key to eternal salvation.

As with mathematics and philosophy, so it was with natural science. The Greeks were continually searching for explanations concerning the working of things in nature, and they relied on systematic observation and experimentation. Greek innovations in medicine are perhaps best considered as efforts to explain body functions. The oath of Hippocrates of Cos merged this practical knowledge with an ethical system that has become the ideal of medicine even though it is sometimes violated in practice.

The Greeks investigated other fields of natural science besides medicine. Initially this exploration was religiously guided, for the Greeks viewed religion and the emerging rational "scientific" attitude as not incompatible. Man's rational powers, they reasoned, would eventually discover how the world created by the gods really functioned and would not call into question the gods themselves. However, the basic Greek notion that the gods did not disclose everything to man, and hence man must discover through reason and experimentation all that the gods had not revealed, soon led to agnosticism and atheism.

The Greeks' discoveries in natural science contributed to an inflated sense of accomplishment and ultimately to the great sin of pride. They now began to believe that reason alone was sufficient to unravel the mysteries of the workings of the world and that even the need for the limited and circumspect Greek gods could be erased. It is here that humanism arises, a secular religion of man, elevating man to a false godhood. Rather than using it to guide man to an understanding of the workings of God's plan in and through nature, the Greeks misused reason in trying to explain away their gods.

Although the early Greeks had no descriptive term for what we now identify as the "social sciences," it is clear that their philosophical writings contain much of what today we regard as psychological and sociological explanations of human nature. As they tried to explain the physical world rationally, so they applied reason to human conduct. Their theory became an *ideal,* and the concept of the "rational person" as the "ideal person" is a heritage left to us by the Greeks. All that could not be rationally explained became known as "irrational" and "false." This turning of rational scientific explanations upon man himself left room only for the natural rather than the supernatural. And here we finally find the true origin of what ultimately became Darwin's evolutionism—a purely rational explanation of the origin of man, constructed within natural scientific theories.

Eventually Greek rationalism, like the Greek imagination, contributed to the country's decline, for rationalism extended beyond its proper limits becomes itself a source of error. Our legacy from the Greeks has been absorbed all too well in this respect: the merely rational individual is an incomplete person. It is therefore not surprising that this legacy sowed the seeds of agnosticism and atheism so rampant in modern Western civilization. Mythical tales of Greek gods were ultimately regarded as projections of mankind, as indeed they were. And if the Greek myths were not literally true, might not the Bible itself also be just a collection of other myths, also not factually true? If reason alone is to judge imagination, cannot reason alone judge the Word of God?

The Greek mind, totally devoid of true divine revelation, became merely rational. Reason was elevated to the level of a Greek god in the same way that it has now become the god for the emerging secular humanism of the modern Western world. The Greek mythical tales of life's origin and the origin of the gods were acceptable insofar as they prepared the mind to *seek* purposeful, intentional interpretations of life in a power greater than mere mankind. Their myths failed however, because Greek rationalism discovered that these tales were just fantasy.

But the Greeks didn't stop there! They embarked on a venture to unravel the mysteries of the world outside of myth. But they went too far. With their gods dethroned, mankind was placed on an illusionary throne and once again mistaken for deity. The Greeks had indeed learned to see the error of their belief in *mythical* gods, yet true conviction was lacking; to fill the void, their pride led them to believe that they themselves were now the gods of their destiny.

The Greeks were masters in the use of imagination to forge tremendous human achievements, but this does not mean that their historical accomplishments were as phenomenal as is often thought. On the contrary, the "Glory that was Greece" lies solely in the eye of the beholder.

The much-heralded unity of the culture belied the political disunity of rival city-states. They shared in common a single dominant language, a strong dislike for the barbarians, an appeal to their man-created gods, "divine sanctions" by the priests and priestesses of the oracles, but these in themselves did not create a united nation. The unique unifying factor was not language or culture or a shared religion, but rather the Olympic Games. In the mistaken belief that their gods loved games, the Greeks held athletic competitions every four years in honor of Zeus on the plain of Olympia in Elis. So great was their desire to accommodate the gods that the starting date for their own history was made to coincide with the date of the first Olympiad in 770 B.C.

Representatives participated from every city-state. Only Greeks could compete, and on the jubilant heads of the victors was placed the esteemed olive wreath. Commerce thrived around the games. Greece became united—temporarily—as one people in competition. Wars were even halted so that the games could take place.

But why would mere games be such a vital ingredient in the development of so great a nation? Perhaps they unified the country as nothing else could. Yet this superficial solidarity fell apart the moment the games ended. At that point the bitter hostilities that had been suppressed for the duration of the games erupted all over again because of the diversity of the people inhabiting the islands and mainland states.

When we think of Greece, we invariably see the words "Sparta" and "Athens" slip before our mind's eye. They represent something we tend to forget. The Spartans, history tells us, were a hardy, bellicose people who conquered the area of southern Greece known as Laconia, making the city of Sparta its capital. The Spartans kept the original inhabitants as slaves because of a constant fear of reprisals. The Spartans regarded only themselves as people of substance and responsibility, and consequently only they were allowed to participate in the political process. But since this city-state owed its existence to violence, its only survival was by the sword. Children were reared under harsh conditions with all males fated to be warriors. In fact, a council of sages passed judgment on each newborn male child, banishing the apparently weak ones to die. All common labor was anathema to male Spartans. They were bred for war, lived for war, and died for the same cause; but life even without war was rigorous and austere. Spartans inhabited rough-hewn homes, survived on tasteless broth, and had to achieve superior feats of prowess. No wonder they looked forward with great anticipation to the Olympic Games, for it would confirm the superiority of their system.

By the middle of the sixth century B.C., the Spartans were the major power in the land of Greece. They applied the sword to their own citizens in the same way they applied it to their conquered neighbors. Here, in the midst of a civilization so admired by the Western world, we find a portion of its people ruling by fear, force, and the sword—a militaristic society to a degree perhaps unmatched by any subsequent civilization. Maybe they were less imaginative than other Greeks, but they were certainly just as rational. The Spartan way of life produced a nation of fierce warriors, unaffected by either altruistic ethics or a true faith; yet, to be a warrior and conquer even the entire world only leads to destruction, for without a soul no nation can endure.

Sparta was Greece without a soul. . . .

Turning to Athens, we discover a different Greece—the Greece of mythical proportions that is emphasized in most of the history books. Athens was a land without slaves in which democracy was the guiding force. It was the Greek imagination at its best. All forms of the arts reigned supreme as a free people conducted their business of exploring the limits of human imagination. Yet, despite this overwhelming aesthetic appeal of Athens, her gods of marble remained all too human, and her imagination became impotent in the face of gods who appeared little more than giant men.

Simultaneously, while the philosophers walked the streets of Athens jostling the minds of the passers-by with their appeals to mere reason, the impotence that had attached itself to their inventiveness and artistic ability now also began to gnaw at their reliance on reason. It quickly became apparent that reason alone was limited and that it had reached its ultimate boundary. The human heart continued to cry out for more understanding, but beyond the sharp edges of reason awaited only darkness.

A comparison of Athens and Sparta shows the paradoxical nature of ancient Greece. In one area existed the unyielding militarism of Sparta, ruling, living, and surviving by the sword; and at the same time, another region of the country was guided by imagination, culture, and reason. That these contrasting city-states eventually clashed violently in the great battles of the Peloponnesian War is perhaps prophetic in its own way. It signified the downfall of both states, for history records that at the Peace of Nicias in 421 B.C., the Peloponnesian War ended and a fifty-year peace ensued without a definite victory for either side. Both survived but were severely weakened and ready for national death—and it remained for Alexander the Great to salvage the remnants of Greece before the eventual onslaught of the Roman Empire.

Greece in retrospect presents us with a mixed yet meaningful lesson: " 'Not by might, nor by power, but by my Spirit,' says the LORD Almighty" (Zechariah 4:6). Indeed, not imagination nor reason nor military might alone can guarantee the survival of a nation, no matter how great. If these factors contributed to the ruination of Greece, then how much more are they applicable to Western societies unified only by relentless desires for economic expansion and political supremacy? Yet today, the age-old warning goes unheeded. The limits of reason and imagination, as well as ruthless might, confront us once again. God has been left out, and no nation has ever survived outside the Word and the will of God.

Chapter Six

The Grandeur That Was Rome

Whᵃt was true for Greece is applicable to Rome, for in many respects Rome stands as *the* challenge of history. Not only do historians continuously debate the conditions that eventually led to her fall, but they are divided as well concerning the conditions responsible for her rise. Indeed, many civilizations have not lasted as long as it took Rome to fall.

Rome is of special interest to us in that many Americans of this generation see the United States as the Rome of the twentieth century. If this is a valid comparison, then we may have to face the realistic assumption that America may neither last as long nor fall as slowly as the Roman civilization.

But Christians look beyond the political aspects connected with the rise and fall of Rome, because to them she stands, above all else, as the civilization into which the Messiah was born and to whom the vacillating Pontius Pilate surrendered the only true Christ for public execution. Rome's rejection of Christ—and consequently of God—is both prophetic and historical. Because of this intertwined relationship of political decay and turning from God, one questions whether America, caught in its current trend of indifference to God and drifting toward a growing reliance on heathen supernaturalism, can survive.

In most of the great civilizations of antiquity, a combination of scientific, historical, and mythical knowledge provided a multiplicity of contradictions regarding their origin. In this respect Rome was no different. Her beginnings remain a matter of controversy and differing viewpoints.

The historical record shows that in about 300 B.C., Roman justice found the bankers of Rome guilty of charging excessive interest rates on loans. As punishment, all their fortunes were confiscated and designated to be used by the public works commission to enhance the appearance of the city. One project financed by these funds was a bronze statue of a wolf suckling two infant boys. Today this statue, now reconstructed, stands as a monument to the legendary founding of the empire. The importance of this statue, erected in perhaps 296 B.C., is its testimony to early Rome's need to affirm her origin.[1]

The difficulty in attempting to trace the birth of Rome arises from the fact that written Roman material dates from approximately 500 B.C., while most of the records dealing with Rome's early history are found only in Greek writings dating to about 750 B.C. No matter where we glean our information, the precise beginnings of Rome are likely to be forever obscure.

Most school children learn the legend of Romulus and Remus, the two male babes who were raised by a she-wolf and survived to found the civilization that eventually became Rome. Yet, the early history of Rome is intertwined with that of the Greeks, and historians consider it highly plausible that Rome was not founded just once, but twice!

Rome was established in an historically glorious time when Greek heroes bravely traversed the seas, and it is therefore not surprising that according to the Greeks, it was one of their heroes who founded Rome. Even Roman historians gave credence to this myth and acknowledged that it was either the sons or grandsons of Aeneas, a wandering Greek, who founded a settlement called Lavinium on the Palatine Hills near the river Tiber. These relatives of Aeneas, Romulus and Remus, are credited with the first founding of Rome. The settlement, however, died soon after.

The second founding of Rome occurred when, as the Greeks tell it, Aeneas's son Ascanius left Lavinium to establish a settlement to the southeast known as Alba Longa. There, the legends say, the sons of Ascanius, Numitor and Amulius, fought a pitched battle, resulting in Numitor's being driven from power. Not satisfied with his victory and wanting to eradicate all potential influence of his deposed brother, Amulius took the twin infant sons of Numitor's daughter and set them adrift on the Tiber. It was these two boys who were supposedly found and nursed by the she-wolf after their basket was marooned in the soft mud left by the receding river. According to the legend, passing shepherds ran off the she-wolf and raised the boys to be herders of cattle and swine. Upon reaching manhood, Romulus and Remus were eventually reunited with Numitor, and upon judgment from the gods, Romulus was chosen to found a new city on the Palatine Hills. Using a sacred stick to mark the initial boundaries, and following with a paired bull and cow to plow deep furrows along the landmarks, the outline for the city of Rome was thus established.

Whatever the exact date, and whether or not Rome did have a second founding that began with the "furrow of Romulus," history, not legend, relates that the scattered villages on and around the Palatine Hills near the Tiber ultimately joined together in

753 B.C. into a single city-state under the rule of a "king." Some 153 years later, the swampland below the hills was drained, and the first Roman Forum became the meeting place of its citizens. But while Rome's history can undeniably be linked to a single source, the Tiber, the origin of her people is as diverse as the many tributaries that feed that famous river.

Historians may dispute the veracity of the "Romulus furrow," but relevant facts do support the idea that on the approximate site of the "second founding," there lived numerous peoples with manifold talents. These formed the nucleus of the great city. What eventually would characterize the Roman citizenry—a bellicose nature, a pastoral orientation, a fiercely patriarchal allegiance, and a hedonistic private life—were all characteristics contributed by peoples already thriving before the founding of Rome.

From the nomadic and pastoral people of the Apennine Mountains came the effective use of iron and the tools of war. These people are historically verified to have occupied the site of the future Rome as early as 1350 B.C. From the Etruscans, a problematic people of disputed origin, came the pragmatic appeal to simple humanism that was to express itself in the private, pleasure-seeking lives of the Romans.

From the Greeks came much of the "sacred canopy" for Roman culture. They brought writing to the Romans, and indeed, early Roman history is available only through the eyes of the Greeks, due to their mastery of writing. Greek gods, so very human, became Roman gods, often with only a change in name. This mythology combined with Etruscan influence to make Rome a chiefly humanist-oriented culture masquerading under the guise of a multifaceted polytheism.

The Mediterranean shores supplied the more physical features—the short limbs, the dark, kinky hair, and the deeply tanned skin—that gave Rome and eventually all of Italy the basic "Italian stock." These people, probably driven from Africa due to the decimation of the great Sahara Desert, existed about

1500 B.C. in the area where Rome was to be. Other peoples such as clusters of Indo-Europeans supplied the Roman language with a firm linguistic base. Combine this with the iron weapons and the bellicose nature of the Villanovans from the north, and Rome had all the ingredients to become a powerful military machine that was to spawn its own civilization.

A city and a culture emerged that was fated to unite Italy into "the grandeur that was Rome." Soon after the fusion of these diverse people, the building of the city began.

The historian Paoli has compiled some truly impressive statistics about Rome.[2] At the time Constantine transferred the capital of the Roman Empire to Byzantium in the fourth century A.D., Rome covered an area approximately twelve miles in circumference. Eleven aqueducts supplied the city with a seemingly unending stream of crystal clear water, reaching a magnitude of perhaps 350 million gallons a day. Because of the superior workmanship and superb engineering of these aqueducts, many survived and are still in use today.

According to Paoli, Rome's bustling traffic entered the city via 29 major highways, which inspired the adage "All roads lead to Rome." In addition, numerous minor roads crisscrossed the city and cut it into *areas* or small "parks." Eleven major bridges were so well constructed that they are still regarded as marvels of engineering. But that wasn't all. History and archaeology tell us that the city had 2 large markets, 11 forums, and 10 basilicas. The architecture of Rome was impressive indeed and included more than 1,300 fountains, 37 marbled arches, a circus, amphitheaters, and no less than 28 libraries. In keeping with the Romans' reputation for cleanliness, 11 public and 856 private baths were also built. It is therefore understandable why history books today speak of grandeur in Rome. In sheer architectural mass and impressiveness, no city in history can be compared to Rome, the "Eternal City."

In the earliest known periods of Rome's history, her citizens were a simple, hardworking, pastoral people, continually threat-

ened by the river Tiber. Gradually, as the tree-clad hills around
Rome were cleared and swamplands at the base of the hills were
drained, Rome took on a new character, but problems remained.

In the fifth century B.C., King Servius built Rome's first protective wall, within which were overcrowded buildings chiefly of
wood and weak forms of limestone. The early city was forever
fragile, and if the waters of the Tiber did not rot the beams or
soak the soil upon which the buildings rested, then fire, Rome's
other natural enemy, took its toll.

Fire threatened Rome as inevitably as the river, not only because of the wooden construction, but also because Rome itself
was situated in an earthquake zone. Records reveal that in 213
B.C. and again in 192 B.C. the city was nearly destroyed by fires
caused by earthquakes. Firefighters with crude leather-sewn hoses
were impotent in the face of such catastrophes.

Other fires in Rome's early history are more suspect. The great
fire of A.D. 64 at which "Nero fiddled" damaged no less than ten
out of fourteen divisions of Rome. There are indications that
Nero, thought to be its chief arsonist, wanted to clear the major
center of Rome in order to build his famous "Golden House."
When the house and its surrounding features were finally completed, it was so mammoth that Nero's successor Tacitus is said
to have complained that there was little left of Rome beside it.

Rome's enemies also added considerably to the city's "fiery
history." The Gauls, for example, literally reduced the city to
ashes in the fourth century B.C. Thus, between the harassment of
invading armies, the ravages of nature, the unpredictable Tiber,
and the ever-present fires, the "Eternal City" was in a constant
state of change. It is no wonder that the early Romans were seen
by the ancients as a pragmatic, practical people who led a simple
life—in between fighting for their very existence. Surprisingly
enough, however, from this population of mixed breeds, loosely
knit bonds and varied customs evolved a strong feeling of unity
and determination. The inhabitants of the great city were fast becoming one people, all sharing an aggressive and warlike nature.

As Rome began to wage war and embarked on the road to expansion, its character began to solidify. Clashes with Greece in southern Italy and wars with Sicily in the First Punic War some 250 years before Christ brought Rome into contact with the great Greek architecture. This fact, combined with the discovery of extensive marble deposits, inspired the Romans to copy Greek buildings. Within a relatively short time, all the old Etruscan temples were replaced by Greek-styled marble edifices that would endure far longer than the Roman Empire itself. Much of the marble discovered by the marching armies of the empire was rapidly transformed into functional structures. It supplied the building blocks for the Marcian Aqueduct constructed in 144 B.C., and the river Tiber was arched by her first stone bridge as early as 142 B.C. Gravel roads were covered with stone. So extensive was the use of marble that Emperor Augustus would say—with some accuracy—that he "had come to rule a city of brick and had left a city of marble."

Yet the achievement of Augustus lay in more than gleaming stone. A capable administrator, he defined the city limits and, through an innovative system of government, presided over a Rome divided into fourteen major regions with a magistrate appointed to govern each. These larger units were subdivided into numerous smaller districts, and the voting populace elected forty-eight *magistri* to govern them.

In many other ways as well, Rome was highly advanced even by today's standards. Each region, for example, had assurance of a medical doctor to care for the people, and police were employed whose paradoxical function was mainly to fight fires. At various growing periods in Rome's history, walls were built around the perimeter, giving the appearance of a city in which walls within walls served both to define and protect its inhabitants. Often, holes were made in the walls to facilitate pedestrian traffic to other sectors of the city, yet its center was still the Forum. By 179 B.C. all the shops in the Forum were united into the Marcellum, a major "business-shopping complex" suggestive of our modern shopping centers. As population pressures mounted, other Forums were built alongside and around the initial Forum so that like the larger city of which they were a part, Rome had Forums within Forums—a labyrinthian complex containing most of the business and social life of Rome.

If there was a heart to the city of Rome, it was the Forum. Paoli has provided extensive and poetic descriptions of life in this pulsating center. The diverse peoples comprising Rome's population were fated to mass together there, displaying both their virtues and vices; suggestive of many modern cities, the pressure of a rapidly increasing population made the Forum, as the inner heart of Rome, the place where the best and worst was evident. Perhaps it was all the more evident as the gradual expansion of Rome by assimilation of its neighbors combined with the conquests by the Roman legions of various peoples with their different customs and traditions.

The contradictions within Rome grew. At the time of Caesar all wheeled vehicles were prohibited in the Forum areas; consequently thousands of Romans interacted freely in these densely crowded areas. Here operated the moneychangers and the beggars, and here the living carried the dead. And as with modern cities, the territories and its inhabitants changed drastically within relatively short distances. Fine homes dotted the hills on the outskirts of the Forum areas, while thousands of the poor and desolate slept the nights away under bridges or in hidden crevices in the walls of the city.

As Rome became fortified with walls, embellished with marble, and ambitious for empire, her citizens began to pay a heavy toll. Ultimately it affected the family structure of the Romans, a critical consequence.

There is a considerable degree of unanimity among historians regarding the strong role of the family in early Rome. It is perhaps more true of Rome than of any other civilization in ancient history that her actual might rested upon the firm and secure family structure of its citizens.

The Roman family unit was built on a powerful paternal authority in which the male dominated the household, while the woman held dignity and respect as wife, mother, and educator of the children. Lower-class Roman marriages were based upon a dowry system. Most marriages in the early Republic were religiously sanctioned. A wheat wafer, shared between wife and husband, sealed a ceremony that united the couple for life. Divorce was virtually unknown among the Romans, and the need to replenish huge war losses was only one of the many reasons that having large families was encouraged. The very security and structure of the family encouraged both man and wife to rear many children, both as expressions of their love and, equally important, for the ever-growing needs of the Republic.

Fidelity in marriage was the accepted norm among Roman families. Strict yet principled discipline was administered by the father, while the mother had charge of providing basic practical and moral training for the children. A husband had the right and obligation to kill both man and woman caught in the act of adultery. Sexual fidelity was expected even of slaves.

Philip Van Ness Myers notes,

> It would be difficult to overestimate the influence of this group [the family] upon the history and destiny of Rome. It was the cradle of at least some of those splendid virtues of the early Romans that contributed so much to the strength and greatness of Rome, and that helped to give her dominion of the world. . . . It was in the atmosphere of the family that were nourished in the Roman youth the virtues of obedience and of deference to authority. When the youth became a citizen, obedience to magistrates and respect for law was in him as instinct and indeed almost a religion. And, on the other hand, the exercise of the parental authority in the family taught the Roman how to command as well as how to obey—how to exercise authority with wisdom, moderation, and justice.[3]

But if the family was Rome's strength, religion was its weakness. The Greek gods were larger than life, but the Roman gods were more humanlike. Some Roman emperors even declared themselves to be gods and were worshiped as divine. It is not surprising that the Romans rejected the only true God and carried out the crucifixion of His only Son.

As Rome expanded, she acquired a diversity of gods borrowed from different sources. Congruent with Rome's military expansion was the god Mars, known as Mars the Avenger, who was thought to be a combination of warrior and pastoral caretaker, uniting Rome's imperialism with her earlier pastoral origins. Mars himself had a Greek parallel in Ares, and it is likely that the Romans simply borrowed this god from the Greeks. The gods of Rome had no myths associated with their origin as did the Greek or Etruscan gods, but rather, like all things Roman, even their gods were pragmatically employed. Mars the Avenger presided over Rome's battles and her preparation for war, for if Rome was not engaged in war, she was preparing for it.

Another of the many gods was Vesta, again probably borrowed from the Greeks. She was conceived primarily as protector of the hearth and of the Roman home. A temple to this goddess stood in the Forum to remind the citizens of her concern for the family; it was impressive indeed, built from marble and patterned after the Greek style. To assure its influence throughout the realm, an eternal flame was maintained in the temple by six vestal virgins chosen for this sacred task in childhood and destined to serve for thirty years. While the rituals associated with these virgins are perhaps strange to us, in them the explicit awareness by the Romans of the sanctity of the family was affirmed.

Jupiter was a god above all gods. He too was borrowed from the Greeks, who called him Zeus. His symbols, the eagle and the thunderbolt, were immortalized in marble and in the practical activities of the Romans.

The gods represented a crude form of worship in which men were seen as gods, but in time, the average Roman began to distrust these gods and wondered about their very human nature. Because of their disillusionment, mystery sects from the East held great appeal for many Romans, who were searching for the obscure rather than the obvious human qualities in their gods. That the true God would eventually walk among them in human form, be adjudicated by an angry mob, and be crucified with the approval of the Roman government was a mystery that would later shake the very foundations of the empire. Yet, for most of Rome's history, she had the gods she deserved—simple, practical deities whose main function was to ensure the military prowess of Rome abroad and the social stability of Rome at home.

As it was with Roman gods, so it was with Roman ingenuity. The pragmatic mind of the Roman was always scheming and planning, which resulted in the rise of a technology as impressive as it was limited. Again, borrowing from diverse cultures, the Romans took tools and ideas and adapted them to their own needs. On the one hand, technology was fostered to further Rome's military might; on the other, she used her captured wealth to make improvements at home that depended upon an advanced technology. The famous aqueducts are but one example, but there are many others. Rome used the water wheel for power and invented a water heating and cooling system that found use in the most expensive homes. A large number of Roman roads are still serviceable today, and buildings still stand as impressive monuments to the greatness of Roman technology.

But the technology had limitations. Being practical-minded, Rome cared only for what would permit or facilitate military expansion and satisfaction of hedonism at home. So even though Rome's outward appearance was superior by any standard, inwardly the limits of humanism were discernible. Consider Roman law, the empire's crowning achievement. Just as Greek is the initial language of philosophy, so Latin is the initial language of law. The renowned historian Will Durant once described Roman law as "the most characteristic and lasting impression of the Roman spirit,"[4] and indeed it is. Yet, in Roman law we also see the fallacy of trying to construct a legal system in purely rational terms. Early Roman law had the right of force only, and as Rome expanded, she imposed her rules upon others; this rule of force became the precedent upon which the Roman jurists had to structure a system of law and "justice" *responsive* to change.

The bedrock of Roman law lay with its citizens, who initiated requests to the Senate to be made into law. Here we have the foundation for a republic in which individuals elected by the people decide on new laws. Roman law could also be initiated by magistrates and even lesser officials, who announced new rules with respect to civic matters by posting them in the Forum. Ultimately the law was derived from Rome's rulers, with Caesar, for instance, making radical changes and Augustus introducing a completely new constitution. Underlying it all was the conviction that Roman law was to be an expression of universal principles applicable to everyone; but even though the laws were adopted and universally applied, their validity was forever in question because their source was merely human.

Rome had no appeal to any transcendent source for law or morality, and hence it fought over basic rational principles—a Greek pastime that the Romans adopted as a kind of verbal sophistry. The only two sources of Roman law were the citizens, who had legal power to express their opinions and were the originators of the law, and second, the Roman family governed by the father, who as head of the household represented a strong source of power in his own home. Not surprisingly, however, his influence in the family decreased as the power of the government increased. The goal of Roman law still exists today, which is the universal application of principles derived from the people and applicable to all in equal measure . . . the ideal of a purely secular philosophy.

The "profession" of law was nonexistent until late in the years of her decline. Initially law was studied as a civic responsibility, and men wise in the law advised and defended others strictly for matter of prestige. Under the system, it was illegal to levy fees, though often after a case, the defendant would voluntarily bestow a gift upon his defender. Only when the apparent futility of rules and regulations rooted in fallible human sources became evident did "lawyers" and "law" as a profession emerge, with lawyers then charging for their services. Soon Roman law became, like all secular law, a game of regulations and loopholes, played for high stakes regardless of any real moral concerns—a sign of decay, not of justice.

In summary, this was Rome: an expanding civilization that overcame its own geographical limitations, uniting a major portion of the known world by force, appealing to "human" gods to perpetuate their might, and reaping the benefits of brute militarism at home in the forms of hedonism. The family units constituted her real strength, yet ultimately this strength too was directed toward purely secular pursuits.

Here then, in the building and maintenance of Rome, we find the seeds of her destruction. That Rome fell is a fact of history; but exactly *why* she fell is perhaps the most disputed question of history. Edward Gibbon, the classic historian of Rome's decline, has said it can be considered the "greatest, perhaps, and most awful scene in the history of mankind." Indeed, for many, Rome's demise is a final and fearful warning to any civilization that claims for itself indestructibility.

Great civilizations do not tumble at once. The same factors that created Rome's greatness undermined her as well. With critical eyes, historians have examined the various stages of Rome's decline, and from these a number of vital elements must be emphasized.

First, Rome's response to the physical forces that threatened her was purely technological and in no way spiritual. Her citizens were unable to restrain the Tiber that, with harsh regularity, overflowed its banks in spring and summer, drenching the marshy banks, undermining the foundations of massive marble monuments and making them sink under their own weight. The wooden houses that the newer marble, limestone, and concrete structures replaced had long since rotted away. The sewers that served to drain the many valleys along the river were technological marvels but could not avert the ceaseless forcefulness of the water.

Another continuing threat was fire. The great fires that raged time after time within Rome's walls left massive arches standing naked and destroyed the most combustible metal, wooden, and brick structures. Hence, as Gibbon notes, Romans were haunted throughout their history with charred reminders of their failure to create permanency. Today, silhouetted against the Italian skies, the skeletal remains of a once-opulent Rome stand remote and crumbled, hollowed out by time and ravaged by the elements—a witness to the futility of her materialism.

Second was the utter failure of Rome to follow either her own legal codes or the moral code provided by the presence of Judeo-Christian religion. The early laws of the country were built upon fundamental general principles of human rights shared by all people. But to insiders, Rome's basic legal problem was obvious. Without a firm basis in an ultimate source or divine code of ethics, the laws enacted by the Senate and dictated by the emperors were quickly reduced to "merely laws," meaningless *guidelines* that were changed and modified whenever a contending group protested loudly enough or whenever current mores demanded looser reins. The diversity of the Roman population assured that no simple rational system of legal codes was possible. Even less was achieved when in desperation Rome finally turned to her gods, for with their human attributes they became a source of aggravation rather than salvation. Indeed, as emperors stood to affirm their own divinity, Rome was taking the final steps on the road to national destruction. With emperors becoming gods, religious constraints were abandoned, and Rome evolved into a meaningless society.

To a Roman in the "best days" of the Republic that preceded the empire, religion represented stability in the state and in the home; it was the foundation of public and private life.[5] These "best days," however, were destined to end. The decline of Roman society had long since progressed beyond possible reclamation by the time Emperor Constantine declared Christianity the new state religion in the third century A.D. A.H. Jones comments, "For the vast majority of ordinary men Christianity caused no fundamental change of attitude."[6] There is every indication that the idea of a universal religion received widespread support, but nominal acceptance of Christianity did not really alter the basic nature or lifestyle of the empire's citizens. In fact, any Christian moral teaching seems to have made little practical difference. Religiously speaking, Rome soon became a melting pot of values, with different systems of religious faith vying for supremacy.

"The old beliefs were *not* forsaken in response to the challenge of a more profound understanding of higher spiritual values," writes E.B. Castle, "but merely because they failed to satisfy intelligent people. When the appeal of a higher moral purpose is absent, men seek their own sensual satisfactions."[7] Other historians draw the same conclusions. Jerome Carcopino writes,

> The Roman pantheon still persisted apparently immutable.
> . . . But the spirits of men had fled from the old religion; it still
> commanded their service but no longer their hearts or their belief.
> . . . In the motley Rome of this second century it had wholly lost
> its power over the human heart.[8]

It was this loss of spiritual power that increased the Roman's vulnerability to disruptive influences. By living a religious life without real conviction, the searching hearts of Rome were once more introduced to the superstitions of the East. Sun cults and mystery religions seeped into the empire and fused with the remnants of the Roman religion and the principles of Christianity. They came from Persia, Syria, and Egypt, brought to the shores of Italy by foreign traders, slaves, travelers, and soldiers who were returning from long campaigns in distant lands. It was this complete distortion of true religious principles that led Rome into confusion and turmoil, affecting every facet of her existence.

Third, the Roman educational system began to exchange *goals* for *values* and failed to inspire its youth to prepare and discipline themselves to meet the problems of the nation.

Contrary to later developments, well-defined goals and values were integrated into the educational system of early Rome. It was formulated to meet the demands of responsibility toward the family, the community, and the nation; it prepared to confront realities head-on with strength and ability. Later, in the Republic, under the influence of Greek culture, elementary, secondary, and higher schools of rhetoric and philosophy were established. The latter were based on the works of so-called great pagan authors, namely Homer, because the Romans eagerly coveted the culture of their conquered subjects, especially the Greeks. They established schools patterned after the Hellenistic type to rival those in the East at Athens and Rhodes.[9] But when Rome grew, and wealth and comfort became the goals of life, character building became a forgotten issue.

M.L. Clarke writes,

> The Roman Schools did not profess to do anything more than inculcate a particular brand of learning. They did not claim to build character, to teach religion or patriotism or morality, and some ancient teachers were notoriously ill equipped for such teaching. . . .
>
> Yet there was certainly a feeling abroad that a schoolmaster should be something more than a mere instructor, that he should take the place of a parent, perhaps even supply that moral guidance that some Roman homes conspicuously failed to provide.[10]

Another prominent historian expresses the thought: "The moral, social and intellectual climate was not healthy; there was no grand conception of the education of the whole man."[11]

Much has been written about Rome's final years, but few authors have penned as much or as eloquently concerning the demise of Roman education as Jerome Carcopino, who, in his book *Daily Life in Ancient Rome*, unreservedly points out the following:

> On the whole we are compelled to admit that at the most glorious period of the empire the schools entirely failed to fulfill the duties which we expect of our schools today. They under-

mined instead of strengthened the children's morale, they mishandled the children's bodies instead of developing them, and if they succeeded in furnishing their minds with a certain amount of information, they were not calculated to perform any loftier or nobler tasks. The pupils left the school with the heavy luggage of a few practical and commonplace notions laboriously acquired and of so little value that in the fourth century Vegetius could not take for granted that new recruits for the army would be literate enough to keep the books of the corps. Popular education then in Rome was a failure![12]

The neglect of education resulted in a succession of developments that accelerated the speed with which the empire declined. What the conquered saw of Rome belied her internal deterioration. "Under the brilliant exterior of the Roman Empire," comments Rostovtzeff sadly, "we feel the failure of creative power. . . . We feel the weariness and indifference which undermined, not merely the culture of the state, but also its political system, its military strength and its economic progress."[13]

Fourth, Rome had outgrown its early stages. The empire literally burst with wealth and fortune. But the "easy life" that characterized so much of Rome during its years of military and economic supremacy had its own built-in dangers. As one historian notes,

> The "Pax Romana" brought many blessings; it made possible the greatest luxury, the most active commercial life the world ever saw. . . . Though a few savage tribes might ravage the frontiers, the quiet interior provinces were destined to perpetual peace and prosperity. . . .
> And so in this dream of the absolute fixity of the Roman system, men went on getting, studying, enjoying, dissipating— doing everything to prepare for fighting. . . .
> The excessive desire for wealth without regard to methods or to duty toward posterity . . . the downright sensuality were accomplishing their perfect work. The economic evil was at the bottom. First Italy, then a vast Empire, devoted itself for centuries to a feverish effort for getting money by any means, and to spend that money on selfish enjoyment. Other things went for little. . . .[14]

The cost of maintaining the "peace of Rome" soon proved too expensive even for the wealthiest of nations, and Rome's remarkable resources were too limited to support all that this expansion demanded. Drawing a straight parallel between conditions in Rome and the United States, Gov. Ronald Reagan of California pointed out the following facts in an address he delivered at a fund-raising dinner for Eisenhower College in 1969:

> History tells us that Rome had a pioneer beginning not at all unlike our own pioneer heritage. Amazing, however, that even though it took two centuries to reach its pinnacle of greatness, its decline started when the empire entered its third century—but the tell-tale signs of political and moral decay were already apparent in the latter years of the second century.
>
> During those years, we are told, there were vast increases in the number of the idle rich as well as the idle poor. The latter were put on a permanent handout, a welfare system not unlike our own. As this system became part of the political scheme, the recipients of public compassion increased in number. They even formed their own political machine with sizable power, and were not at all hesitant about making their demands known, . . . nor was the government reluctant to give in to their desires, . . . this with ever-increasing frequency. The rich catered to them, would-be emperors bowed down to them, and as a result, the great solid middle class of Rome—the country's strength—was taxed more and more to support a bureaucracy that kept growing larger and more powerful. Surtaxes were imposed upon incomes to meet emergencies. The government was forced to embark on a policy of deficit spending, and the denarius, a silver coin similar to our half dollar, began to lose its silvery hue. It took on a copper color as the government reduced its silver content. . . .
>
> Military service was an obligation highly honored by the Romans. In fact, a foreigner could win Roman citizenship simply by volunteering for service in the legions of Rome. But with increasing affluence and opulence the young men of Rome began avoiding this service, finding excuses to remain in the soft sordid life of the city. They took to using cosmetics and wearing feminine-like hairdos, and even used "unisex" garments until it became difficult, historians tell us, to tell the sexes apart. . . .
>
> Among the teachers and scholars of ancient Rome was a group

known as the Cynics, whose members let their hair and beards grow and who wore slovenly clothes and professed indifference to worldly goods as they heaped scorn on what they called "middle class values." As a result of this, the morals declined; it became unsafe to walk in the countryside or the city streets. Rioting was commonplace, and sometimes whole sections of towns and cities were burned to the ground. And all the time, the confiscatory taxation and creeping inflation were growing and waiting to deliver the deathblow.

Finally, the combination of indifference, moral decline, and greed won out . . . and Rome fell!

Whether or not there is a fifth factor in the fall of Rome rests on a question still debated by many historians: "Did Christianity contribute to Rome's downfall?" The question apparently arose when the dust of the crumbling empire had barely settled, because St. Augustine wrote his classic *City of God* essentially to show that Christianity did not.

One point is indisputable. When the tenets of biblical Christianity are used to pass judgment on Rome, Rome is found wanting and doomed to destruction.

Some facts are obvious. The initial Roman rejection of Christ is biblically and historically confirmed. Herod's vain effort to kill the God-child (Matthew 2), Pontius Pilate's abandonment of Christ's fate to "people's judgment" (Matthew 27), and events in between demonstrate Rome's defiance of the true God. But beginning with Christ's resurrection, the spreading of the Word rumbled throughout Rome and intensified the shaking of her already weakened foundations. Amid the death-throes of the empire, Rome persecuted the Christians and used them as Colosseum bait in an attempt to obliterate the growing dissent. Yet Rome's fight was not really against the Christians, but was rather an attack on God.

If there was a way in which the Christians contributed to the fall, it was in their disengagement from Roman social and public life. Worshiping the unseen yet omnipresent God, they purposefully avoided helping to build temples and monuments to honor the emperor's deities. Indeed, as Rome entered her final decline, it was the Christians who helped destroy those buildings dedicated to human gods and goddesses, realizing then as well as now that governments must be supported only insofar as they pursue and foster God's will upon earth. Caesar ignored the claims of Christ on the human heart and instead forced his citizens to render all to *him* . . . and Christians boldly refused.

Today Rome literally sits upon her own ruins. She has become a skeleton of her own past and a reminder to us all of the destiny of a civilization without a soul.

Chapter Seven

Is There a Formula for Decline?

We have shown that history supports the general thesis that as civilizations rise, so must they fall. It has been said repeatedly that civilizations last on the average no more than two hundred years, but those we have examined went far beyond that time span, for they are among the greatest in history.

What nation today can match the glory of Greece at the height of her power? What nation today can equal the grandeur of ancient Rome? Where is the nation that can surpass the tremendous might and staying power of the proud Egyptians? And where today do we find an empire with the beauty and architectural splendor of Babylon?

Nevertheless, our task is not merely to recite facts contributing to the rise and fall of empires. In the final analysis we have to examine the lesson that is to be learned from historical developments. Two errors are common today among those who claim to have learned the lesson of history but who in reality own nothing but sophisticated ignorance.

On the one hand are those prophets of doom who tie historical processes in with so-called iron laws of rise and fall, supposedly operating totally outside the control of mankind. These analysts draw carefully devised parallels between fallen civilizations and America and arrive at the solemn conclusion that nothing can be done to save America—especially since she already has embarked on her "inevitable" decline.

The fallacy of this line of thought is that, while one can point to a recognizable pattern of decline, there is really nothing "inevitable" about the process. Civilizations *can* control their collective destinies up to a point, within God-given limits, and the very recognition of the process of decline can be used to identify the measures that have to be taken to reverse the trend. Hence, we shall avoid being simply prophets of doom, while at the same time admitting the harsh reality of America's cultural decay.

On the other hand are those who misapply biblical wisdom and suggest that since the Christian must render unto Caesar's that which is his due, he can absolve himself totally from responsibility for the historical processes as if God cared nothing about purely "secular" matters. This error leads toward political apathy and escapism. It is error to imagine that the Creator of this world has no further interest or involvement in the affairs of this globe or with the historical development of civilizations. The prophetic chapters in the Book of Daniel clearly point out the fallacy of this line of reasoning.

As we have emphasized before and shall again, God's plan for human beings involves their collective existence as well as the destiny of each individual, and therefore God simply cannot be unconcerned with what people do as community and society.

The question that confronts us is, What can be said concerning the rise of empires that is relevant to us in the twentieth century? What can really be learned from the fate of the former empires that we have examined? And most important of all, what is the accumulated lesson of history, left to us as a legacy from the fallen empires who now cast only shadows of their former greatness?

We have stated already that a major criterion of cultural greatness is the character of a nation's people. Sociologists dispute the concept that society is merely a collection of people; but it is nevertheless true that the nature of a people ultimately determines the nature of their culture. In this sense, Reisman's analysis of character, mentioned earlier, is again relevant. Ultimately the character of a people is crucial, not only to the health of the individual, but to the health of his culture as well. To a Christian, the nature of mankind must be acknowledged as forever rooted in God's plan, and hence there are biblical constraints on both man and his civilization that are intertwined. Most simply put: *It is the degree of obedience to God's will that is the ultimate criterion of success.* Question: How can this obedience be applied to the rise and fall of civilizations?

Toynbee[1] has provided a massive overview of history, pointing among other things to the various factors contributing to the rise and fall of civilizations. While he does not use expressly biblical criteria in his analysis, he is most sensitive to the spiritual issues involved in his subject. Much of what he claims in general spiritual terms can be applied in specific fundamental biblical terms. This is particularly true in the role of adversity.

Toynbee has argued that great civilizations have arisen largely as a response to *adversity*, rather than, as many might suspect, a response to easy or at least tolerable conditions. The Egyptians confronted the great river Nile and gradually built a major civilization in response to her foreboding challenges. Likewise, Rome rose beside the Tiber and relentlessly responded to her periodic rage. The point to be made is that harsh geographical conditions invariably require cooperative responses aimed at a common goal in order for a great culture to arise. Survival against the adverse circumstances of nature comes as a result of a cooperative effort. Yet this is not without its drawbacks, for the effect of this survival venture is twofold: It severely limits individual rights and calls for denials on the part of the individual, forcing him to bear significant burdens for the good of emerging society; and it also exploits the labor and efforts of the individual. Hence, cooperation breeds exploitation as emerging nations use the division of labor to benefit "power groups."

The initial rise of civilizations under inhospitable geographical conditions unites the populace only temporarily. Cooperative harmony among peoples toward a common goal begins to fail precisely when the goals are achieved. Thus we can expect a civilization to show the first signs of decay at about the same time the goals are achieved. The paradox of this is that common, pragmatic self-interest is insufficient to bind a people together. What is needed instead is a spiritual bonding that can be achieved only with a common goal based upon shared and ultimately binding ideals. These ideals are revealed for the Christian in biblical revelation. Until that moment in history when the Word became available, civilizations could only approximate this spiritual binding through false and incomplete gods.

As a technical response to seemingly insurmountable odds, Egypt and Rome stand as perhaps the most successful challengers to the forces of nature. The people of the "two Egypts" of the upper and lower Nile learned to seek a common source, the Nile, for the common good. Yet to make the Nile a god was to personify a natural process in an unnatural manner. The Pharaoh became a living god, and the unification of the two parts of the country in terms of this spiritualization of their response was directly dependent upon the power of this god; but because he was a god without godly qualities, the nation bequeathed failure. The ultimate message for Egypt was clear: Monolithic truth, guiding the destiny of mankind, must not be allowed to degenerate into false philosophy and false doctrine.

Rome made the same mistake. Her growing strength arising from her conquest of the Tiber and the geographical conditions of Italy led to the worship of numerous gods under the command of the "god of all," the Emperor of Rome. Yet as the Romans soon learned, the designation King of Kings could not be applied to one who was proven to be merely a man among men. Eventually, there was rendered to Caesar that which was truly his—the decay of the Roman Empire.

In previous chapters we have seen how Babylon and Greece also decayed from within. Greece unfettered the reason and imagination of mankind, but created faint abstractions of her gods, whose humanness was all too apparent. Babylon treasured her false gods as guiding forces, using them as a front to mask the deceitful intent of her rulers. Here too the initial response to the challenge posed by hard environmental conditions led to the rise of great civilizations, but at the same time sowed the seeds of their eventual destruction as well. Ancient history shows that a people united only for conquest and material self-interest is a people fated to build their own collective tomb.

As a second step that correlates closely with the rise of civilizations in the face of commonly confronted hardships, we should take a look at the development of technology. It is a mistake to identify technology only with assembly lines and machinery, characteristic of what has so often been termed the Industrial Revolution. Technology is best identified with the systematic utilization of techniques to achieve a consistent end. This being the case, we can recognize that the ancient civilizations were equally as "technological" as our modern nations; our surveys of Babylon, Egypt, Greece, and Rome have indicated their extraordinary technological achievements. Yet civilizations *cannot* be judged and considered great solely in terms of their technological development, for it is precisely this development that helps lay the groundwork for decay.

To conquer the Nile and to build the massive pyramids required an innovative technology. Many say that our own technology cannot duplicate the building of the pyramids because their method of construction still remains a mystery to us. Their construction required a specific technique applied in the context of the historically advanced technology of ancient Egypt. But while we marvel at the pyramids as a technological achievement, their value remains minimal in terms of spirituality. A fanciful and fallacious belief in an afterlife guided their technology, architecture, embalming, and numerous crafts—but where did it lead them?

The Scriptures present us with an appropriate response to the desire for worldly possessions, technology, or control of human nature.

In Luke 4:5-7, we are told of the devil's temptation of Jesus Christ in these words:

> The devil led him up to a high place and showed him in an instant all the kingdoms of the world. And he said to him, "I will give you all their authority and splendor, for it has been given to me, and I can give it to anyone I want to. So if you worship me, it will all be yours."

This passage focuses on the issue at hand. The Devil offered Christ the promise of technological command over the world of matter, for the promise was that *if* Christ would worship the Devil, then He, Christ, could rule *this* world.

But Jesus responded decisively and rebuked him saying,

> "It is written: 'Worship the Lord your God and serve him only'" (Luke 4:8).

This reaction is the historical Christian response, for conquest and technology are irrelevant, and by implication *harmful*, if not directed toward the service of God.

What then should be our evaluation of the great technological civilizations?

Mere material development, unguided by spiritual demands, is not to be confused with advancement. Indeed, a nation may "progress" technologically while losing her very soul in the process. This principle can be traced in all former great empires. Will eventually the same be said for modern America, the most technologically advanced nation in history?

J. Herbert Fill has provided us with an instructive American parallel to the great pyramids of ancient Egypt. He casts an inquisitive glance at New York City's World Trade Center, a monument to perhaps the latest in twentieth-century technology. The twin towers of the skyscraper loom 110 stories high—1,353 feet. What the majority of people see is an impressive building complex; what Fill sees is a giant machine—a technologically sophisticated, yet impotent robot, which someday may be viewed by future historians as an imposing example of material achievement and spiritual decadence as well.

In the World Trade Center, Fill points out, only one person is needed to monitor the computer control of the building complex, which creates such intense internal heat that it requires 100,000 gallons of water per minute just to keep it cool. More than 6,500 remote sensors feed the computer information on humidity, temperature, water flow, and power needs that "animate" the complex. The computer regulates all these systems and can even kick in alternate generators during "brown-outs"—periods of high energy demand that drain the electrical supply—and shut down the entire system should it be necessary.

No one can deny the significant technological inventiveness that went into the construction of the skyscraper, yet when the question is asked why it was built—why have a complex of approximately nine million square feet that overshadows even the pyramids—only vague answers are given. After probing for meaningful responses from the people and sources closely connected with the Trade Center, Fill's conclusion is an ironic comment of the debatable "might" of modern technology: "The reasons for the center's construction are still obscure. Not hidden, but just unclear to all."[2]

At least the Egyptians had a clear, even though misguided idea of the purpose of *their* pyramids. We don't as yet for ours.

Again, technology is a two-edged sword. On the one hand it permits partial control and modification of the material world for human ends; on the other hand it *cannot* serve to illuminate or guide the ends that should be sought. Furthermore, naked technology ignores the spiritual dimension of human nature. Technology gives us the illusion of freedom, advancement, and control, when in fact it only traps us into submission. No civilization rooted in the Devil's temptation of Christ and the promise of material control can delude itself that it is under the protective umbrella of God's plan. Hence, technological "advancement" is not a sign of progress in any spiritual sense, and a culture devoted to technological "solutions" is destined to be blind to spiritual insights and can never be great. Its very material success belies its spiritual disease and potential death. No nation can survive without a spiritual soul.

If we regard the scientific effort to harness nature and the environment as an ultimate factor in contributing to cultural decline, then we must also acknowledge that in a strange psychological fashion, these efforts can *themselves* be forms of "cultural defense mechanisms," obscuring problems of a more fundamental nature. For instance, as we have already seen, Rome continued to advance technically even after cultural decay had begun. It is almost as if the material concern with modifying the basic form of society allows nations a temporary postponement from facing their mounting spiritual problems. In this sense, at least, technological advancement may be actually indicative of spiritual decay: *the very desire to "advance" can be an escape effort and a refusal to confront underlying spiritual concerns.*

We have stated repeatedly that the very soul of a nation is rooted in the character of her people. Only when persons genuinely share common values, based on a single source of authority, can we have a united society, cooperatively building toward the future from a position of strength. The values of the civilization must equal those of her individual citizens—the conscience of her people. Furthermore, these values *must* be rooted ultimately in God's plan if they are to have any significance at all.

In this lies the paradox of freedom and constraint.

On the freedom side is the fact that willful obedience is required and, when adopted, serves to meaningfully guide and constrain behavior. On the constraint side is the fact that if not willfully accepted, laws and rules become mere games, acknowledged only by a fear of "being caught." Hence, individual citizens comply only insofar as obedience serves self-interest. Here we find a loosely coagulated clustering of people, not held together by common values, but rather forced to live with one another under the onus of compliance.

That there are serious limitations to this is obvious.

First, as civilizations incorporate diverse peoples into their cultural and national boundaries, value differences become very pronounced. Pluralism emerges, with various groups of different cultural and social backgrounds competing with one another for social power. Usually the dominant group is in control at the outset, but as persons of divergent values increase in number, only brute force can hold them in check. Gradually the civilization begins to lose her ability to restrain them, for now "they" are a power structure, and internal revolt rears its ugly head. In Rome, Babylon, Greece, and Egypt, the expansion of the empires produced a dissipation of strength that ultimately became one of the factors contributing to their downfall—but unfortunately it was not recognized by their rulers until it was too late.

Second, as varied groups of persons establish legitimate power bases in a society, doctrines of relativity emerge. Each new group presents an ideological justification for its behavior and all are given equal credibility. People become "free" to choose among belief systems, and the society in which they live often assumes and maintains a "neutrality." We saw how in Babylon different systems of religion spawned numerous superstitious beliefs; in

Rome, how Roman law evolved into a profession. Likewise, in Greece human reason was challenged with the task of differentiating systems of belief, but it soon became apparent that reason as mere reason can justify *any* belief system. As society rationalizes its own actions and proceeds to elevate human law above God's law, progress is twisted, and degradation and decay result.

Third, as more and more effort is directed toward controlling the diverse people comprising a nation, the use of technological means of restraint grows. The same technology that was first used to combat the natural environment is turned against mankind itself. Soon it becomes necessary to establish institutions to control and contain others, with the uncontrolled seeking subjects to control and the controlled fighting to be uncontrolled. Chaos prevails—and the culture decays!

Closely associated with the loss of control over nature and mankind is the emergence of personal alienation and loss of self-control. Individuals no longer feel secure in a value system based on governmental authority, but seek a relatively safe refuge among those who share like views. Homes are locked by the socially fearful. One person's pleasure becomes another person's fear. Crime becomes a way of life, and society is transformed into a system where there is continued "war of all against all" with the "armies" marching to the tune of unbridled self-interest.

As societies move toward a growing pluralism based upon groups scurrying for power and influence, it is coerced into an acceptance of new ideas. But the effort to construct new institutions also creates problems for which the community is unprepared. Too many poor and unemployed? The Roman reaction was to apply welfare on a large scale. But is it the proper response? Presented as an innovative "solution," it becomes a problem in itself. Bureaucratic behemoths emerge in the name of progress and become cancerous growths gnawing at the heart of society. Individual destinies are now swallowed up in the larger whole of the bureaucratic web—and people are trapped.

Again, the "solution" becomes a problem and another sign of decay.

As civilizations veer away from spiritual norms, men withdraw from a reliance on the Word of God. "Secular" forms of delusion appear as reason becomes rampant. And this Greco-Roman heritage of supplanting God's revealed Word with man's calculating reason is undeniably a negative one. Any effort to ignore the validity of God's Word is automatically accompanied by an attempt to construct a false idol. While one cannot predict with certainty the form of the future of mankind and its idols, it can be predicted that any deviation from God's Word must of necessity be idolatrous; and to a Christian, idolatry and cultural decay are intertwined.

In cultural decay we see the unfolding of what is appropriately defined as *paganism*—the pure worship of self, apart from any transcendental value system. The final idol and false god becomes man himself, and the resulting cult of self-worship appears in all its treacherous forms. Individuals seek diverse forms of ideologically justified self-aggrandizement; as people retreat from God, the immensity of the loss is invariably accompanied by the inflation of self. The result is the same everywhere: a hedonistic, pleasure-seeking society of people whose very plea for self-growth marks the temporality of their civilization.

There are two other indicators of cultural decay to consider. Both can be called "victory delusions"—the first military, the second nonmilitary.

As nations decline, they often become militaristic. On the one hand this militarism is expressed in violent attacks against other nations. Yet this attack often reveals a real inner weakness of the attacking nation—a nation too weak to rule and lead and hence compelled to use violence as a last resort. Ironically, if the attacked nation perceives this inner weakness, it will retaliate with even greater effectiveness. The result is that increasing numbers of nations use military force to resolve disputes that could be adjudicated. History witnessed the expansion of Rome until she crumbled under the might of her own armies and was defeated by military forces that were truly her inferior.

Declining empires also use military force to press for solutions to social problems. As an empire weakens, internal problems can be most quickly resolved only with the use of force.

What, then, in summary, accounts for the decline of all major civilizations without exception? The person who fails to heed the call from God cannot grow, but the one who has grasped God's hand must continually ensure that he does not backslide. Similarly, *civilizations who once collectively responded with spiritual greatness still are in danger of losing that greatness if they neglect to live up to their spirituality.* This deceptively simple fact—one that underlies all developmental patterns of the world's leading nations—can be expressed in several ways.

Once again Toynbee provides us with a thought-provoking list of responses to adversity showing that a retreat from spirituality inevitably leads to the death of a nation.

1. *The loss of command over the material environment,* signifying the loss of control over material conditions that results from a cultural breakdown. For instance, the deterioration of Rome's technological achievements in architecture, civil engineering, and art followed the decline of the empire; it did not cause it.

2. *The loss of command over the human environment,* pointing to the myriad ways in which the voluntary social control of cooperative interactions decays, and civilizations are no longer able to protect their own citizens effectively. Even within a given culture, life develops into a "battle of all against all."

3. *The failure of self-determination,* including the progressive inability of a nation to be self-sufficient due primarily to lack of continued spiritual development. Cultural leaders become mere politicians, and individuals participate in and follow their leaders' example primarily for material gains. When this happens, a nation begins to lose its collective soul.

4. *The failure to create new institutions,* which historians see as a

telltale sign of decay—most of them failing to see the importance of maintaining institutions such as the family in their original form. Both the failure to create new institutions and to perpetuate the needed old ones harbors within itself the seeds for national decline.

5. *The worship of false idols,* referring to the point at which civilizations begin to reify and rigidly apply merely material solutions to basic spiritual problems. It is here that outmoded and inappropriate techniques are used as hope for salvation. The claim that "technology will someday solve the problem" or "Congress will find a way" fall into this category. It should be remembered that when civilizations rigidly appeal to institutions and techniques initially established in response to adverse situations rather than to the spiritual source underlying those techniques, then decay is inevitable.

6. *The worship of self,* dealing with the rising egotism of mankind and the belief that past achievements and individual acts of greatness are sufficient for continued and future accomplishment. It includes the foolish claim that "success is individually earned and achieved" and "I alone did it," without recognition of the role of God in individual and collective achievement.

7. *Militarism,* referring to the increasing use of military and forceful means to solve problems. Even when military action is apparently effective, history indicates, the use of force is a sign of decay. To this should be added another dimension: strong-arm tactics used *within* the culture to control its own members.

8. *Intoxication of victory and over-self-reliance,* the nonmilitary parallel to forceful victories. It points to the abuse of legally won power by the nation's institutions and the illegitimate use of political means to achieve the greedy goals of those in power.

These eight criteria of cultural decay are evident in the twentieth century to show that humanity's spiritual response to its fallen state accounts for both the rise and decay of his society. While there is no formula for "rise and fall," civilizations do follow a predictable growth pattern much like that of the human body: birth, growth, decay, and death. Decay grows like a cancer until the culture is ultimately consumed.

The final disintegration of a civilization has always been marked by a number of identifiable historical developments. While historians sometimes define categories and subcategories of disintegration, brevity demands that we condense them into two dominant areas: (1) *schisms of the body social,* and (2) *schisms in the soul.*

Historically the world has watched empire overtake empire, and the rise and fall of civilizations has become a repetitious affair. All followed the pattern of birth, growth, decay, and disintegration, but in every case this last stage did not occur until a society had completely abandoned its reliance on spiritual responses to growing hostile conditions. As this desertion continued, societies were literally torn apart through dissatisfaction, greed, and finally revolt. The elements most responsible for the social disintegration can easily be discerned in the ruins of the fallen empires:

1. *Dominant minorities begin to fight for power among themselves.* The nation is no longer socially or spiritually unified. It becomes merely a collective society where power is the supreme issue. To protect their selfish interests, groups in society vie for political dominance without concern for the damage it may inflict on the welfare of the nation as a whole.

2. *A lack of patriotism emerges in what Toynbee has termed the "internal proletariats."* Huge numbers of people become disaffected from the social system and feel that while they are *in* society, they are not *of* it. Compliance with the law comes only when absolutely necessary and only through fear of detection and punishment. Even within morally sensitive minorities, "political games" become an everyday necessity to ensure their political survival.

3. *Power confrontations lead to the final blow.* Society is no longer able to use its moral and spiritual influence to convince its neighbor nations of its morally justified approach to external

problems, but is forced to resort to power confrontations. Armed truces and stalemates now form the basis for the country's stability, and it becomes easy for smaller and less developed nations to hold the "empire" at bay.

What has been said of the decline in the "body social" is discouraging, but the real indication of a civilization's final disintegration is reflected in the last major category of internal destruction, identified by Toynbee as "schisms of the soul." Inasmuch as Toynbee began to publish his monumental *Study of History* as far back as 1922, there cannot have been any collusion between his historical findings and a critique of more recent developments. Yet the "schisms of the soul" that he identifies after an extraordinary study of twenty-one empires are readily discernible in culture today and full of dire forebodings.

1. *Alternative ways of behaving, feeling, and life.* As a once-great civilization falls apart, myriad forms of behavior, feelings, and lifestyles emerge. Everyone begins to "do his own thing," without firmly rooted styles, mores, or values that used to exist for the majority of the citizens. Nobody knows for sure what to believe or in what to believe. By now any lifestyle is deemed appropriate.

2. *Promiscuity as a way of life.* Social and moral decay is accompanied by a way of life dominated by the vulgar, grotesque, and promiscuous. Sex in all its raw forms runs rampant, and the righteous aspects of man's biological nature are debased and exploited publicly. New forms of sexual abuse replace traditional morals, and family life disintegrates.

3. *Futurism.* Dissatisfied with a multitude of unfulfilled desires, society begins to adapt naive and utopian views, trusting that the new way of life will lead to a brighter future. Tradition now is declared "old-fashioned," and all hope is focused on abandoning it for a "new" way of life.

4. *Alienation and anxiety rule supreme.* The final step on the road to total disintegration is a surrender to feelings of detachment and passivity. National elections lose their voter appeal; craftsmanship has given way to mechanization; welfare becomes

a much-sought-after alternative, rather than a temporary solution or last resort; and people act like anxious robots, moving,
acting, and reacting independently—fighting, lying, and cheat-
ing their way through regulations for personal survival.

Again, in much the same way as we have seen with schisms in
the "body social," the effects of these four major elements of
breakdown are cumulative, each new one drawing strength from
the wreckage wrought by the previous one. When these combine
with the simultaneously developing schisms of the soul, the empire succumbs.

The parallel between the rise and fall of nations and the creation and fall of mankind is significant. Man, expelled from the
Garden of Eden and forever tempted to ignore his Creator, falls
victim to his baser nature time and time again. And as he does,
his culture is dragged down with him. The failure to respond
spiritually to the problems created by his fallen nature is man's
guarantee of eternal damnation. Similarly, within the boundaries
of time, social "collectives" of people who disregard their spiritual potentials take but shortened joyrides in cultures that cannot
stand the stress of time.

Casting a backward glance at the elements that caused the
downfall of the major empires of the past, we find startling
similarities that should serve as a warning to America.

In balance, the picture looks like this:

ELEMENTS OF DECAY AND DISINTEGRATION

Elements	Antedil.	Egypt	Babylon	Greece	Rome
Moral disintegration	x	x	x	x	x
Disobedience to God, false gods	x	x	x	x	x
Collapse of the home	x	x	x	x	x
Pride	x	x	x	x	x
Failure of education			x	x	x
Fratricide	x	x	x	x	x
Reliance on superstition	x	x	x	x	x
Brute military force		x	x	x	x

Elements	Antedil.	Egypt	Babylon	Greece	Rome
Violation of code of laws by priests or governor	x	x	x	x	x
Political indifference		x	x	x	x
Treason		x	x		x
Feeling of oversecurity	x	x	x	x	x
Increasing hedonism	x		x	x	x
Overtaxation		x	x	x	x
High inflation			x	x	x
Large standing army		x	x	x	x
Open lawlessness	x	x	x		x
Overreliance on reason	x			x	x
Lying, cheating	x		x		x
Gross corruption	x	x	x		x
Vice	x	x	x		x
Depravity	x	x	x	x	x
Steadily declining spirituality	x	x	x	x	x
Rejection of the true God	x	x	x	x	x
Too rapid development of technology	x	x	x	x	x
Reliance on success alone		x	x	x	x
Pessimism and cynicism	x		x	x	x
Political disintegration		x	x	x	x
Weakened resistance		x	x	x	x
Economic chaos		x	x		x
Well-oiled welfare system					x
Dependency on allies for mutual defense		x	x	x	x
Slavery, using prisoners of war		x	x	x	x
Hypocritical priesthood		x	x	x	x
Belief in fantasy and myth		x	x	x	x
Extreme rationalism				x	x
Philosophy carried to the extreme				x	x
Agnosticism and atheism	x	x	x	x	x
Political paralysis		x	x	x	x
Avalanche of divorces	x		x		x
Zeal for physical pleasure	x		x	x	x
Mixing of the races			x	x	x
Futurism	x			x	x

Nations and empires have come and gone since the fall of Rome in A.D. 476. Smaller empires have arisen since that time, notably the British, French, and Dutch colonial empires, and in a peculiar way, the United States "empire." With the first three having lost their position as major world forces, our attention should now be directed to the United States, which has become undoubtedly the most influential world power of all time. America is not a colonial power—at least not when we define a colonial power as a nation that has subjugated distant lands for political and economic control. But America is nevertheless the focal point of a far-reaching financial and economic empire, connected politically with countries around the globe by more than forty treaties and alliances.

What is the trend in America? Is she following in the foot-worn tracks of her greatest predecessors, and will she perhaps also crumble under the same forces that caused their decay and disintegration? Or does she possess sufficient moral and spiritual fiber to ward off the process of decline and fall?

Chapter Eight

The Death Cry of an Eagle

That past empires have followed one another in relatively-quick succession and have entered their final convulsive days in very much the same way is a matter of historical record.

We cannot speak of a precise formula for "decline and fall," for human society does not act according to the ironclad laws of physics. However, the pattern of decline has been repeated so often and become so predictable that many social scientists are seriously beginning to question whether the United States as the world's "leading democracy" will be able to avoid the merciless cycle of history and "remain" glorious, great, and indivisible.

I put "remain" in quotes, for even though it was only a few

years ago that concerned voices were first raised by world leaders, calling into question the complexities and changes of modern life, we are now no longer just *approaching* the brink of disaster; we have *arrived. . . .*

Kenneth J. Holland, editor of *These Times,* comments,

> . . . The common man senses that something unusual has happened, and he fears that he is fast becoming unable to handle life. Students at the University of Maryland, when interviewed, stated that mankind has lost control of things, has lost any leadership it had, and that we are heading for some kind of world-wide catastrophe. *A surprisingly large number felt that the next great event facing humanity will be the second coming of Christ!* [italics ours].[1]

Many may not want to believe in the possibility of Christ's second coming, but if it is the "next great event," then we are now living during a time when the next-to-last great event is taking place—and judging from the concern voiced by leading journalists, statesmen, and social scientists, this event may well be the death throes of what is known as "the American civilization."

"What is still called Western civilization," writes the distinguished British journalist Malcolm Muggeridge, "is in an advanced stage of decomposition." The lifestyle and happenings up to and through the Bicentennial of the United States have brought this harsh assessment sharply into focus.

Something has indeed happened to the West and to America in particular. The shifting tide of political, economic, and military affairs, coupled with the revolt of the masses against moral norms thus far held sacred, has made America "different"—at least different compared with the way she was.

Don't get me wrong: she's still a grand old lady, but her appearance is somewhat tattered, and her step has become erratic and unsure. Things have changed in America, and no one should realize it better than herself.

We have indeed come a long way since milk was 9 cents a

gallon, a shave at the local barber cost 3½ cents, and the United States numbered only two life insurance companies instead of today's 1,821. Things have changed, but should this transformation have been so traumatic? Cries of alarm sound throughout the land, from all strata of society.

Attributing our current problems to the disadvantages inherent in our system of government, U.S. Senator Daniel P. Moynihan has stated, "Democracies are becoming a recessive form of government, like monarchies used to be—something the world is moving from, rather than to. We've taken enough punishment lately to wake ourselves up and realize *we may be in trouble*" [italics ours].[2]

Samuel P. Huntington, political scientist at Harvard University, blames our own actions for this "crisis" syndrome. He feels democracy has gone too far and sees a potential danger in this:

> It [the democratic process] is healthy only up to a point. It has unfortunate consequences in that it's very hard to put any sort of limits on the process. It feeds on itself—thus tearing down institutions, tearing down leadership, tearing down individuals. And it only comes to an end when people *get exhausted. We may be approaching that point now.*
>
> It seems to me that we are moving from a phase of great moral indignation and moral fervor into a phase of rather deep cynicism. I think that is unfortunate. . . . In the past decade, we've swung too far to the extreme of challenging authority, dismantling it, exposing all of its abuses—important and unimportant, real and imagined. *As a result, it's very difficult for anybody to govern this country today* [italics ours].[3]

Echoes the esteemed economist Robert L. Heilbroner of the New School for Social Research in New York:

> All the polls indicate a serious dropping off of public belief in the efficiency and trustworthiness of government. And I don't have to tell you that distrust is multiplied in what are called "intellectual circles." *The mood of the country is not* [yet] *one of black despair, but it is very sober* [italics ours].[4]

America's Bicentennial year and the years immediately following put the spotlight on many of the country's declining values. The values upon which American civilization was built are being reconsidered and found wanting in many respects. Not only are the time-honored virtues of hard work, thrift, self-discipline, self-reliance, sharply defined moral concepts, and love of family and country taking a back seat, making room for corrupting vices and declining morals, but now, too, Americans are painfully aware of the shocking discovery that global power, once thought to be the monopoly of the United States, is fast slipping from this country's grasp. Today U.S. military supremacy is rapidly dwindling, and political weakness has become a byword. There now appears to be no escape from chronic inflation, steadily increasing trade deficits, or bondage to Middle East oil; instead of seeing the light at the end of the proverbial tunnel and "knowing" that somehow there will be an answer, we face mounting gloom. The past two decades have brought with them a redistribution of economic and political resources, both world-wide and at home, and we're not used to it.

"We used to think of this as a lean, free-enterprise country," says Herbert Passin of Columbia University's School of International Affairs, "but we're becoming second-rate as Britain did."[5] The eventual result will be a highly divided, fragmented society of individuals coexisting in a "non-nation" that no longer believes in itself or knows what it stands for in the world.

During 1976, the Bicentennial Year, the outspoken and controversial magazine *Plain Truth* published an article that summarizes our present situation in a sober yet candid way.

> The continued existence of a democracy such as America's depends upon the character of the nation as a whole, not just of its leaders, who, of course, are the product of that very society. Because of this, the founding fathers fostered the concept of "republican virtue," the idea that the citizenry should exercise a fair amount of restraint, self-discipline, and responsibility.
>
> Most Americans today, however, seem oblivious to the direct

connection between personal moral responsibility and the health of the nation as a whole as it moves into competition with other nations and ideologies on the world scene.

The plain fact is, the survival of America is as much, if not more, dependent upon its internal soundness than its external military defense. The example that America and Americans set for themselves and other nations is of equal importance to a "showing of the flag" in the far-flung corners of the world.[6]

Paralleling these thoughts, Jaroslaw Pelikan, dean of Yale's graduate school, claims wryly that the difference between ancient Rome and America today is that back then only a minority could afford to indulge its senses, while today "everybody is entitled to be depraved."[7] The theme of Jean Raspail's controversial book *The Camp of the Saints* is that a society must believe in itself and its roots or it will die. James Burnham makes a similar judgment in his epic book *Suicide of the West*. Burnham is pessimistic concerning America's prospects for survival, as is his literary contemporary Robert Nisbet, who in his recent book *Twilight of Authority* argues that America has already entered a "twilight age" in which authority has been eroded past the point of no return and decline is inevitable.

The first phase of decline is as hard to define as the beginning of conception. The English biologist Thomas H. Huxley in a prophetic statement appears to have foreseen the enigma of our time when, standing before the gigantic seven-hundred-ton Corliss steam engine at Philadelphia's International Exhibition on May 10, 1876, he exclaimed,

> I cannot say that I am in the slightest degree impressed by your bigness or your material resources as such. Size is not grandeur, and territory does not make a nation. The great issue, about which hangs a true sublimity, and the terror of overhanging fate, is *what are you going to do with all these things*? [italics ours].[8]

And what *have* we done? We live in a republic of technology, yet at the same time this republic has become a world of obsolescence. Seventy-five percent of all the information available to mankind has been developed within the last two decades; millions of pieces of information are created daily, with the total amount doubling every ten days. Today's newspaper makes yesterday's paper worthless; old objects are recycled. Daniel J. Boorstin, the Librarian of Congress, comments,

> Most novel of all is our changed attitude toward change. Now nations seem to be distinguished not by their heritage or their stock of monuments (what was once called their civilization), but by their pace of change. Rapidly "developing" nations are those that are most speedily obsolescing their inheritance. While it took centuries or even millenniums to build a civilization, the transformation of an "underdeveloped" nation can be accomplished in mere decades.[9]

Today we're eager to accept change merely to make life more exciting, more exhilarating. Not only can this change lead a developing nation into the community of responsible and self-governing nations, but it can also reduce a nation of self-esteeming men into a cauldron of human degradation.

And only *we* can prevent the end result of that change from being a frightening monster. The late Margaret Mead wrote in *U.S.A. Today*, "Never before has a generation been responsible for the survival of the entire race of man, but that is the responsibility of the present generation of man."[10]

One of the major causes of the breakdown of the Roman Empire as well as other ancient societies was a total disintegration of the family unit, as we have seen with Rome. From the founding of the United States into the twentieth century, the family has been seen as the keystone to both personal and social well-being in this country. According to sociologist Sheila M. Rothman of the Center for Policy Research in New York,

> The fundamental assumption was that the good order of society depended finally on the good order of the family, its ability to instill discipline and regularity in its members. Success of this

mission augured well for the safety of the republic. Failure jeopardized the experiment that was democracy.[11]

However, that view has changed. What Rothman calls the "discovery of personhood" leads often to the notion that happiness rests not with the family unit, but perhaps in opposition to it. A rapidly changing sense of women's proper roles, uncertainty regarding children's rights, doubts about the very worth of having and rearing children, the ever-loosening legal bonds of marriage—all these have called into question, in Rothman's phrase, "the legitimacy of the family."

Opinions as to the future of the American family differ drastically depending upon the liberality of the researcher's background. A recent study conducted at the University of Texas has concluded that the family is *not* "falling apart," but merely "changing." Linda MacNeilage, counseling coordinator at the university's Counseling Psychological Services Center, says,

> I would have to agree that the family is *changing*, but I don't think it is dying or disintegrating. I think essentially what we are seeing is that there are changes in our society which have repercussions in family life.[12]

Norval Glenn, professor of sociology at the university, pinpoints one of the visible changes in the fabric of American family life when he observes that marital instability has increased sharply. Guy Shuttlesworth of the university's Graduate School of Social Work also reaffirms that it's pretty easy to move in and out of marriage relationships today. One pressure working to diminish family cohesiveness, he says, is that we focus too much attention today on things such as companionship, love, satisfaction, happiness—all of which are very difficult to define even under the best circumstances. Yet no matter how we seek to justify divorce, the rate of dissolved marriages is still at an all-time high, and the end of the rise is not in sight. Since 1975, more than a million divorces have been granted annually in U.S. courts, and now there is approximately one divorce for every two marriages per year.

Clifford Rose Adams, professor emeritus of Penn State University, reported in June 1969 that government statistics showing that approximately 28 percent of all marriages end in divorce are actually misleading. He said,

> If you take in annulments and desertions (about 100,000), which are not included, the figure would be nearer 40 percent. Add to this, what we call the morbidity marriage, where a man and woman may continue living with each other just for appearances or convenience while actually hating each other, and you find that only about 25 percent of marriages are really happy. The other 75 percent are a bust.[13]

Tell the children that it's a "social adjustment"; tell them it is merely a "repercussion of family life"—it does not help to wipe away the tears or soothe the heartaches. Far too many couples are splitting up without fully considering the financial and emotional hardships that divorce can inflict. Such hardships are increasing as alimony and child-support laws change, and living alone becomes more difficult for those not prepared for an independent life.

Sometimes the pain of marriage is better than the emptiness of divorce or the pangs of loneliness. Today a sweeping epidemic of loneliness has struck America as a result of divorce, alcoholism, and sex-related problems, and worried psychiatrists now estimate that a fourth of all Americans representing every age have joined the "legion of the lonely." Requests for help directed to the various counseling centers in a number of the major cities of America are increasing at the staggering rate of 30 percent a year. In West Palm Beach alone, 35,000 people with loneliness-related problems call the Crisis Line service each year. A spokesman for the service says, "Our society produces lonely people. Everything is based on success. People are on the move all the time. No one gets the time anymore to build meaningful relationships. I would say that [a full] 50 percent of the people who phone us are just suffering from plain loneliness."[14] Sam Heilig, Executive Director of the International Association for

Suicide Prevention in Los Angeles, adds, "It's gotten to the point where we need an organization based on the Alcoholics Anonymous system. We could call it Loneliness Anonymous."[15]

It may be in large part this searing loneliness—the feeling of not belonging—that accounts for the increase in illegitimate births in recent years. Even though various contraceptives are available, unwanted pregnancies continue to occur. Everyone wants to be loved; and someone to love, to care for. In 1977, the most recent year for which figures are available, no less than 515,700 illegitimate births were recorded in the United States, of which about half—249,800—involved teen-age mothers. And this despite the fact that abortions have terminated millions of unwanted pregnancies since abortion was made legal in 1973.

It may be accepted in some European countries to have children out of wedlock, but in the United States there is still a social stigma attached to it that creates untold hardship for the young unwed parent.

This desperate yearning to "belong," with its all too often disastrous results, is not limited to the impoverished and unemployed. It has invaded college campuses with equal intensity, and there the fear of rejection has added a new dimension to the problem of loneliness.

Statistics indicate that only accidents exceed suicide as a cause of death among college students. The notes left behind tell of utter loneliness and intense feelings of frustration with society. One study reports that

> 32 percent of the college students who die each year die by their own hand and the rate is rising. The same study also tells us that for each successful suicide attempt, there are 10 unsuccessful suicide attempts and that 80 percent of the students who did take their own lives had made at least one previous attempt.[16]

Can it be that these feelings of despondency and utter despair result from the fact that America does not stand for much any more? Russell Kirk, author of *The Roots of American Order*, asserts that all aspects of civilization arise out of people's religion. Yet Americans are abandoning traditional religious values and are living on a humanistic and materialistic plane. We have seen from past civilizations that, without God, no nation can survive. As a nation "under God," to quote the Pledge of Allegiance, the United States became the world's most powerful and influential country; but today, without recognition of the role of the divine in national affairs, this once-proud nation is beginning to decay within.

Perhaps the time has come to take a second look at our spiritual bank account and examine closely the moral precepts upon which our entire cultural system is based. Startling changes over the last few years have drastically altered the face of America. The concept of living a clean, moral life is, for too many, no longer desirable or sought after in today's world. Figures gleaned prior to 1960 indicate that 77 percent of America's youth believed in living a high-principled and virtuous life, but that was before the turbulent decade of the sixties, with all its agony and confusion. By 1973, the 77 percent had already dropped to 57 percent among noncollege youth, and those who attended our institutes of higher education showed a decline from 45 percent to 34 percent. "Moral living," once listed among the "desirables" of American youth, has now been usurped by rock culture, drug abuse, and the sexual revolution.

Before this rapid change, religious values were paramount in this country for decade upon decade. In the early 1800s, the French statesman Alexander de Tocqueville made a now-famous study of democracy in America and penned the following reaction:

> I sought for the greatness and genius in America in her commodious harbors and her ample rivers, and it was not there.
> I sought for the greatness and genius in America in her fertile fields and boundless forests, and it was not there.
> I sought for the greatness and genius of America in her rich mines and her vast world commerce, and it was not there.

I sought for the greatness and genius of America in her public schools system and her institutions of learning, and it was not there.

I sought for the greatness and genius of America in her democratic congress and her matchless constitution, and it was not there.

Not until I went into the churches of America and heard her pulpits flame with righteousness did I understand the secret of her genius and power.

America is great because America is good, and if America ever ceases to be good, America will cease to be great [italics ours].[17]

What *has* happened to America's basic goodness? What has happened to America's religion?

George Gallup found in a recent poll that 33 percent of the nation's Protestant ministers have considered leaving the ministry, and that 13 percent consider the church "irrelevant." Also, approximately ten thousand American priests left the Roman Catholic priesthood between 1968 and 1974, and the "desire to marry," in contradiction of their vows, was their principal reason.[18] This appears to be a reflection—or perhaps the result—of developments transpiring within traditional Christianity. Today Christian beliefs and practices are being replaced by a "religion" patched together from the doctrines of Karl Marx and John Maynard Keynes, with perhaps a liberal dose of Sigmund Freud thrown in, and this has transformed the religious make-up of the country, revealing itself in the church habits of the nation.

While belief in psychic phenomena is increasing, church attendance is steadily declining. A survey published in February 1975 reveals that education significantly affects church attendance. The statistics tell us that 45 percent of college graduates attend church somewhat regularly, compared with 38 percent of high school graduates and 39 percent of those who have completed only grade school. With less than half of the population attending church and engaged in Christian activities, we certainly have the right to question whether we can still claim fidelity to our Christian origins.

The aforementioned survey has caused considerable conster-
nation in Christian circles, yet Sterling Grey, then president of
the New York-based National Council of Churches, was not at
all disillusioned by it. "A lot of people who don't go to church
are acting out their faith in other arenas—politics, unions, civil
rights organizations and education," Grey rationalized.[19] But a
union hall, a civil rights meeting, or a political rally is not the
same as a sanctuary for worshiping God. Realistically speaking,
only 40 percent of Americans attend church somewhat regularly,
29 percent go occasionally, 6 percent attend on holidays only,
and 25 percent never set foot inside a church building.

In *Pagans in the Pulpit*, Richard S. Wheeler makes some
pointed observations regarding the possible causes of this condition. He asserts that throughout history, liberal theologians have
consistently endeavored to draw people's attention away from
God and bring it back to mankind. He says,

> As a general rule, liberal Christians have abandoned the older
> theology of reconciling unruly man with the will and purpose of
> God. The more modern theology begins with the proposition that
> God is a handy genie who helps individuals to use all their talents
> and resources to advance to comfortable economic levels and a
> measure of recognition in the community. Theirs is a man-
> centered religion; the church exists as a social agency; the clergy
> function as psychiatrists, counselors, and perhaps county exten-
> sion agents.[20]

It is not surprising therefore that Clyde Nunn, sociologist with
the Center for Policy Research, found in America today a declining certainty even about the existence of God. After survey-
ing 3,500 people, he discovered that the percentage of people
who believe merely in the *existence* of God had dropped from 77
percent in 1964 to 69 percent in 1975.

The United States has become a nation where millions are
unfamiliar with even two books of the Bible, but if asked what
their astrological sign is, three out of four can tell you. "The basic
concepts fundamental to religion, such as God, holiness, right-

eousness, sin, grace and love are virtually nonexistent in contemporary academic conversation and discussion," says Harold K. Schilling.[21] If this is true—and we don't doubt the validity of his statement—then *something* must have filled the void. That something is a return to absolute paganism—a belief in the powers of the occult, superstition, and devil worship . . . certainly many miles off the well-principled road paved by our Founding Fathers. No longer is faith in the supernatural limited to the country folk who, needing sun and rain for their crops, often pleaded with the "gods of nature" for a measure of divine intervention.

"Today things are different," many people say. "Science has taken the place of our former superstition. Their actions, however, belie their words, for the affluent in society are now lending their minds and their prestige to the extraordinary growth of modern supernatural phenomena. The Second World War was a dramatic time when faith in the Unknown was suppressed by the harsh reality of bombers, cannon, and breadlines—not to mention the screams of the tortured and the groans of the dying. Stark brutality assaulted the senses, and prayer rose freely from stricken consciences. It is not that superstition was not present, but in most cases faith in God, not in the occult, furnished the strength necessary for survival.

But with the ending of the tension and travail of such a war, a superstitious faith in the power of supernormal events has burgeoned. Since the sixties—the onset of the "Age of Aquarius"—this "new" religion has suddenly become so dynamic and unpredictable that it is no longer socially acceptable to speak of these modern happenings as manifestations of the "occult." Correspondence courses are readily available in psychic phenomena and Satanism; for the inquisitive seekers of diabolism, witches' Bibles and satanic Bibles can be purchased at most bookstores. Psychic seminars and satanic pleasuredomes now dot the land, and some major universities have met the mushrooming demand for occult knowledge by offering bachelor's and master's degrees in witchcraft and sorcery.

The results of these phenomena on our liberated society are obvious.

These practices are conditioning people in general to accept as normal, phenomena that were once considered anti-Christian and as such totally unacceptable in conventional society.

Because of this surging invasion of Dark Power, statistics have undergone dramatic changes. In the United States alone, the number of psychic believers is swelling at an unprecedented rate. As the seventies began, conservative estimates put at approximately forty million the number of Americans in the clutches of the masters of the occult; but the Roper Survey of November 1974 boosted that to 53 percent of the population. Where it stands today is anyone's guess. Sixty-nine percent of Americans now profess considerable faith in astrology and daily consult horoscopes in newspapers. Using the most current surveys as a guide, we know now that not just forty million, as in the past, but 117 million Americans are today being misled by astrologers, psychics, mediums, and clairvoyants. To accomplish this "blanket guidance," 1,250 astrology columns and 2,350 horoscope computers set up in major department stores and shopping centers "program" the nation.

Does this influence our political scene?

You can count on it! While many congressmen and senators do not publicly admit using astrological forecasts in their work, it is big game in the nation's capital. Even local politics are affected by it.

Amassing all supernatural manifestations under the umbrella of "psychic phenomena," Jeane Dixon of Washington, D.C., had forecast,

> Before the completion of the decade [1970-1980], popularity of ESP and psychic phenomena will reach an all-time high. No longer will people be inhibited by what others may say about them; they will have reached the age of experimentation in psychic matters and will probe its depth to discover the power of spirituality. Many will find faith in the Lord through ESP.[22]

Quite a statement coming from a practitioner of the occult sciences who also claims to be a Christian.

The effects of increasing reliance on occult and psychic phenomena for spiritual guidance can be traced in a historical pattern. There is firm evidence that when economic, political, and sociological confusion brings nations to moral disintegration, people flock to mystery cults, begging for answers to satisfy their guilt-ridden consciences. It happened in Babylon; it happened in Athens; it happened in the death throes of the Roman Empire; and the signs appeared in the United States in the turbulent sixties and stressful seventies. Modern man seeks the help of a higher power in times of severe tension or crisis, but today there are no Delphic oracles to consult. But with the abundance of crystal gazers, astrologers, palmists, mediums, psychics, seers, clairvoyants, and devil worshipers, who needs oracles? When people abandon traditional religious faith and turn to superstitious practices, moral principles are neglected, leading to a desire for the "raw" life—the exploitation of the human body. The "sexual revolution" that began in the sixties is virtually two decades old, and it is assumed that most Americans of the younger generation are growing up in an environment known as the "new morality." Pleasure is the guideline, "living in sin" is no sin, and between consenting adults anything goes. Yet, while some observers have proclaimed the revolution a success, battles are still being fought over what the religious community calls "sharply declining morality."

Little doubt remains in anyone's mind that recent years have brought major changes to the established social patterns of America, most notably a greater openness concerning sex and a liberal acceptance of homosexuality, extramarital sex, and abortion. Not tolerated by "the church," this pattern of rampant promiscuity has created a chasm between those who "do" and those who "don't," establishing a battleground for the social scientists who are always eager to transform the sexual adventures of modern America into cold statistics.

To determine what Americans today really think about current sexual morality, the polling firm of Yankelovich, Skelly and White conducted a survey for *Time* magazine. They asked the participants to make judgments on a series of actions as to whether they were morally wrong or not a moral issue at all. The results were both fascinating and sad, for they clearly indicate a discouraging trend of thinking in the United States today.

When asked whether it is wrong for unmarried teen-agers to have sexual relations, 63 percent replied in the affirmative, but ironically 75 percent of their parents believe they are "doing the right thing" to instruct their teen-age children in the use of contraceptives. Also, according to this survey, a majority of Americans (52 percent) believe it is no longer sinful to live together unmarried—a practice that now includes two million persons in America, more than twice as many as in 1970. Many view "living together" today the way an earlier generation looked on sex among the young who were planning marriage or at least were "in love": not really approved, but tolerated anyway.

The Yankelovich poll further reveals that most Americans *oppose* laws against abortion, homosexuality, and governmental prohibitions on sexual behavior. In fact, a surprising 70 percent endorsed the statement that "there should be no laws, either federal or state, regulating sexual practice." Pornography was the exception, with 64 of every 100 respondents concluding that it is morally wrong; 74 percent went as far as supporting the view that "the government should crack down more on pornography in movies, books, and nightclubs."[23] That still leaves us enough to worry about!

But the statistics are only numbers and percentages testifying to a growing problem. What they *don't* tell us is that *because* of this sweeping permissiveness, at least 600,000 boys and girls between the ages of eight and sixteen become involved in pornography and prostitution each year in the United States, and when these children reach adulthood, their degradation will only increase the problems in today's society. About 500,000 disengaged children roam the hostile streets of America's metropolises, and they have become big business.

Times Square in New York City has become a mecca for runaways and throwaways, and many of the 50,000 homeless, unwanted children who pass through the city every year became a part of the $1.5 billion sex industry there. Some stay, some move on, but Densen Gerber, President of Odyssey Institute Inc., a private organization concerned with various social problems, estimates that throughout the year no less than 120,000 children in the New York metropolitan area are involved in some type of sex-for-money, including prostitution. Plagued by hunger, pain, disillusionment, and a need for companionship, homeless youths wander the streets and alleys of more than a hundred of our largest cities, controlled by pimps who are in turn controlled by organized crime. In the last three years, more than two hundred prostitutes have been brutally murdered in New York City.[24] An untold number of others committed suicide.

But New York is not alone. Sgt. Lloyd Martin of the Los Angeles Police Department, testifying before a congressional hearing on legislature to curb child pornography, pointed out that in his city, where he heads a special five-detective squad to investigate sexual exploitation of children, "every year up to thirty thousand children and teenagers pose for pornography." At the same hearing, U.S. Rep. Robert K. Dornan denounced the Los Angeles area, his home, as the center of the U.S. pornography industry. He said,

> This county [Los Angeles] is perverting this nation with the vilest material that's ever been seen by man. This county leads the nation in distribution of hard and soft core pornography, bestiality, sadism, masochism, bondage, and discipline and child pornography.[25]

Officials in San Francisco may want to disagree with Representative Dornan, for it too claims to be the porn capital of the nation. There the problem is completely out of control, and prosecutors have simply given up on the idea of combating it. To many, however, pornography is innocent escapism, a healthy device for fantasizing, a safety valve for dangerous impulses, and a useful antidote to puritan attitudes. Alan Dundes, Professor of Folklore at Berkeley, argues that it is "an informal part of the nation's sex-education program . . . the way American culture prepares people for sexuality." To social psychologist Douglas Wallace of the University of California Medical Center, porn is needed to bring sexual pleasure to the losers in the sexual game—the shy, the unattractive, the crippled. "Are you," he asks, "to deny these victims of our socialization process the satisfaction they might enjoy from looking at these kinds of stimuli?"

Robert J. Stoller, a psychiatrist at UCLA and author of *Perversion, the Erotic Form of Hatred*, makes a pointed two-edged observation when he reasons that "porn disperses rage" that might otherwise tear society apart, but it also threatens society by serving as propaganda for the unleashing of sexual hostility.[26] It is this hostility that we are now facing.

But there are other forms of sexual deviation that deface the nation, particularly homosexuality, which, because of the Gay Rights Movement, has attracted more attention in recent years than more violent forms of perversion such as masochism, rape, and sadism. Even the hundreds of thousands of child-abuse cases compiled yearly in the United States have not received as much notice as the battle for gay rights. Blatant homosexuality has always been associated with the decline of moral values in past empires, and in the United States too it appears that we have "proudly" joined their ranks. Homosexuality since time immemorial has evoked feelings from repugnance to sheer bewilderment, and even though there have been mixed reactions in the past, our nation has never been so confused on this subject as it is today.

Generally speaking, there has been a marked increase in the tolerance of homosexuality in this country since the 1960s when an aide to President Johnson was forced to resign for committing a homosexual act. The kind of public outcry calling for the resignation then might be missing today. Publishing of homosexual materials is running at an all-time high, and gay bars and bathhouses now operate unprotested in communities large and small with so little interference from the police that it almost borders on reverence or respect. Although sodomy laws are still on the books in many states, the desire to enforce them is very weak.

The most basic and solid opposition to homosexuality comes from the evangelical Christian community. To Christians, homosexuality is a sin. In fact, in the Book of Leviticus it is referred to as "an abomination," but right in line with the decline of Christian values in this country, homosexuals argue that Christ himself would have endorsed homosexual mating if his culture had enabled him to envision Christians incapable of being attracted to the opposite sex. Despite the biblical rejection of homosexuality, some major Protestant denominations now permit homosexuals to pastor churches.

If Bible teachings concerning homosexual practice are ignored, and we are encouraged by our culture not to regard it as immoral, then what may be the views of psychiatry and psychology?

Let's take a look at the facts as they confront us now. *Time* magazine reported,

> In a highly political compromise, the American Psychiatric Association adopted a statement [in 1974] declaring that "homosexuality, per se, cannot be classified as a mental disorder." The operative term *per se* left homosexuals free to think that they had been declared "normal," and traditional psychiatrists free to think that homosexuality, though not a disorder itself, was or could be a symptom of underlying disorder. To compound the confusion, the Association felt that it had to list homosexuality somewhere, so it created a new diagnostic category, "sexual orientation disturbance," for homosexuals dissatisfied with their sexuality. This diagnosis can only be applied with the patient's consent. It is a bit like dermatologists voting to ordain that acne is indeed a skin blemish, but only if the sufferer thinks it is.[27]

Though the APA vote seems to have pushed a great many therapists toward a more benign view of homosexuality, a strong body of psychiatric opinion still insists that homosexuality reflects psychic disturbance. A recent informal poll of twenty-five hundred psychiatrists showed that a majority believed that homosexuals are sick. Yet present laws and general tolerance now allow these individuals—thanks to the Gay Rights Movement—to man our pulpits, teach our children, formulate our laws, and act as civic administrators. Is biblical counsel to be taken so lightly? Rome apparently thought so, and that empire was swept into oblivion.

Up to a point, the sexual revolution is closely aligned with the drug culture, violence, and national apathy—all issues we share with the ancient civilizations that slid so quickly into the historical abyss. If the trend being established in this country remains unchecked, we may yet become the most sex- and drug-oriented society the world has ever known. Drugs, especially the so-called "soft drugs," are identified with the American way of life, leading millions of users, particularly in the under-thirty group, to debility and more often death.

While there are ample warnings against the use of substances such as heroin, cocaine, LSD, angel dust, etc., the indulgence of marijuana is so extensive that 43 million individuals already use it regularly. Add to this the 92 million Americans who consume alcohol on a regular basis and the 65 million users of tobacco, and it becomes quite apparent that the "eagle's" claw is reaching menacingly toward America's self-destruct button.

The causes of this behavior are complex, yet most sociologists equate an increase in personal freedom with the many problems in today's society. It is a recognized fact that both historically and cross-culturally, the greatest amount of deviation and irresponsibility in social behavior has always been found in those nations that pride themselves on having more personal liberty. Free nations draw heavily on their right to be different, but once the withdrawal has been made and the vault is empty—then what? Our freedom, similar to that enjoyed by the Romans, seemingly knows no boundaries; but all over the United States, people are beginning to wonder if the waves of assault and battery and homicide that sweep over us are signals of an alarming transformation in the American way of life with no indications of a reversal. Is our morality going bankrupt?

We are following in the tracks of the ancients by moving into the realm of moral irresponsibility; a breakdown in family life; substantial reliance on occult phenomena and parapsychology; sexual deviation—all of which propel us eventually toward a *personal* moral breakdown. Frightening is the fact that this declining phase of life here in the United States not merely affects our reputation abroad, but has led to such a flagrant disregard for human life that in the years 1972-1974, more civilians were murdered in the cities of America than there were U.S. soldiers killed during the war in Vietnam! Our freedom is guaranteed—but is this to be a freedom to kill?

England, with its individual liberty and somewhat homogeneous population, still has a manageable crime rate, as does Japan. Martin Wolfgang, author of a tape entitled *Violence as a Learned Response,* claims that homogeneity is important and promotes a social bond and collectivity—a sense of all of us being alike and together. He further asserts that in the highly heterogeneous countries like the United States, the pluralism of ethnic groups tends to promote separateness, anonymity, and alienation; furthermore, the "subcultures of violence," as he calls them, are the result of friction arising between groups with values at odds with those of the larger society. In those groups, he contends, resorting quickly to physical combat as a measure of daring, courage, defense, or status seems to be a cultural expression. And these "expressions" are certainly manifesting themselves in abundance in the United States.

It is reported that an Asian official once asked Norval Morris, Dean of the University of Chicago Law School, for a foolproof way for his country to avoid joining the nations having high rates of juvenile crime. "Just make sure your people remain illiterate, backward, hopeless," replied Morris, "and confined to their isolated villages for most of their lives."[28] What he said is nothing new, for the French sociologist Émile Durkheim (1858-1917) mentioned crime as an essential feature of a developing society and a predictable by-product of rapid social change. We are now some six decades beyond Durkheim, and his prophetic words haunt us. We're faced with a problem of extraordinary magnitude. Much of today's crime is connected with ideological or political violence, linked to underground movements or other antiestablishment groups, less visible perhaps than in the sixties but no less real.

Contemporary sociologists usually blame America's excessive stress on the unfulfilled promise of material gain or, as proposed by Harvard's Seymour Lippset, the bitterness of being a failure in a society that is supposed to offer equal opportunity to all. But frustrated goals by themselves are insufficient explanation; it becomes a question of whether it is more profitable to work toward these goals or to break the law. Harvard Professor James Q. Wilson suggests in his book *Thinking About Crime* that the benefits of work and the cost of crime must increase simultaneously. To increase one and not the other makes sense only if one assumes that young people are irrational. In an interview with the editors of *U.S. News & World Report*, psychoanalyst-sociologist Ernest van den Haag credited both legal curbs and the decline in religion with the staggering crime rate in the United States.

> Our law-enforcement agencies, unfortunately, are hamstrung at the present. If you have a group of people bent on social violence, it's impossible—no matter how many policemen you have—to stop them unless you have informers within the group, and the courts have made it very difficult to have such informers. These curbs should be eased. . . . [Also] the family, which used to be very influential, has lost much of its cohesiveness and authority.

The trend toward shifting parental responsibility to public institutions, starting with child-care centers, must be stopped. Basic moral education, I think, can only take place in the home.[29]

Van den Haag places part of the blame on the spiritual emptiness found in so many of today's churches.

Churches need to give people something to believe in. One reason for the growth of cults is that the traditional churches have become so feeble. People want more, and it's up to the established churches to become more meaningful to people. We must try to help people gain a personal outlook on life that makes it meaningful.[30]

Whatever cause we accept as the one primarily responsible for the destruction of the moral fiber of the nation, we live with the symptoms, and they are undermining our trust in our fellowman. Of all the crime statistics being compiled at an ever-increasing pace, homicide figures are the most reliable. More than 20,000 persons were murdered in the United States in 1974 alone. Traditionally murders have been crimes of passion or the result of quarrels between family and friends. This, however, is changing. As far as police can determine, 34 percent of the 1,554 people killed in New York City in 1974 did not know their assailant. In fact, 65 percent of all violent crimes committed nationwide are against strangers.

Because violent crime affects all strata of the population, it is almost impossible to guard against becoming a random victim, since it is difficult to draw a profile of the "average" criminal. But *this* is known: Almost half of all the persons arrested are teenagers or young adults. The peak age for violent crimes is fifteen, and 44 percent of the nation's murderers are twenty-four years of age or younger. The nearly three thousand juvenile courts and judges in the U.S. are wringing their hands over the dilemma they face, for the recidivism rate of offenders who are sent to training schools at a cost of more than $23,000 per year per offender is a staggering 80 percent. As more and more judges choose training schools in lieu of harsh sentences for offenders, the young criminals reappear in court time after time. The judicial system has become a joke for the lawbreaker who has little risk of punishment.

Demands for personal security in metropolitan areas is at an all-time high. Professional security guards are never in need of employment, and the guards hired for banks and office buildings often have police background. Denver, for example, has more than 2,500 private policemen as compared with the official police force of 1400 men. Nationwide the army of private guards supplementing the efforts of overworked police departments nearly equals the number of police officers.

But to the citizenry of the United States, this is not enough. As a further means of protection, an increasing number of Americans are forming vigilante groups, reminiscent of years past. In many residential neighborhoods of major cities, men come home from work, hurry through their dinner, and in order to safeguard their families from becoming crime statistics take turns with their neighbors in patrolling the streets.

In our two-party political system where conservatives and liberals battle it out in the halls of Congress, there are as many opinions about how to cure the nation's ills as there are members in the House, with the conservatives favoring the view that it is not desperation but *deliberation* that lies at the room of the problem. Today, however, ideologies relating to the sources of crime are giving way to the realization that the perpetrators of violent crimes must be punished *regardless*.

Former Philadelphia Mayor Frank Rizzo once said, "A conservative is a liberal who was mugged the night before!"[31]

The ultimate problem is one of declining morals. It is all too apparent that the abiding values and restraints that have strengthened and sustained this nation for so many years are now battered and bruised by wars, riots, assassination, racial strife, youth rebellion, strikes, and economic uncertainty. Gross disillusionment prevails, and fewer Americans look to the churches for their moral guidance. Watergate has greatly tarnished the golden shine of America's eagle, and Washington's credibility gap is ever widening. Undoubtedly many of today's observers tend to agree with the nineteenth-century French criminologist Jean Lacassagne: "A society gets the criminals it deserves."[32]

At this point in time, America has managed to equal earlier cultures in the movement toward self-destruction. To reiterate a number of Toynbee's major issues responsible for the decline of a nation: (1) we have lost our command and control of the *material* environment; (2) we have equaled the ancient empires in losing our control over the *human* environment as well; furthermore, (3) we have adequately demonstrated our lack or failure of self-determination as the nation has begun to lose its "soul" and spiritual leadership. But there's more. Toynbee also argues that (4) the failure to create new institutions and the importance of maintaining institutions in their original form, such as the family structure, also play an important role in the demise of empires; while (5) the worship of false gods, a reliance on superficial solutions; (6) the worship of self; (7) militarism as a means to solve problems; and (8) intoxication of victory also contribute heavily. We can add to these the exploitation and misuse of our natural, physical environment.

Winston Churchill, concerned about the march of history, once remarked, "We seem to be moving, drifting, steadily against our will, against the will of every race, and every people, and every class, toward some hideous catastrophe. Everyone wishes to stop it, but they do not know how."[33]

The apostle John writes in Revelation 11:18:

> "The nations were angry;
> and your wrath has come.
> The time has come for judging the dead,
> and for rewarding your servants the prophets
> and your saints and those who reverence your name,
> both small and great—
> and for destroying those who destroy the earth."

Here John is declaring that God will intervene in the affairs of nations and that the divine rule will begin at a time when the nations of earth are incensed and when man is about to destroy the earth. Have we arrived at that point in history? This book is not a study of biblical prophecy, but significantly something is happening to our planet that has never before taken place, and unfortunately the United States takes center stage in the world's final agonies.

When will it all end, if it will indeed end?

A prominent ecologist, Kenneth E. F. Watt of the University of California, gloomily predicts that at the rate mankind is going, we could consume and pollute our way to oblivion by the end of the twentieth century. Basing his pessimistic view on the alarming rapidity with which our modern technological society is consuming earth's limited natural resources—together with overpopulation, the continuous pollution of land and atmosphere, and misuse of what remains—he feels that we are preparing our planet and specifically our American civilization for extinction.

That prediction is rather foreboding and frightening, but many responsible scientists agree that this is exactly what may happen! Ecologist Barry Commoner pointed up the alternatives confronting humanity when he stated that we have just a single decade in which to design the fundamental changes in technology *if we are to survive.* Lee A. Dubridge, addressing a United Nations conference of leading experts on human environment, comments, "Our spacecraft called Earth is reaching its capacity."[34] He might just as well have said that man's destructive nature has finally caught up with him, for we have obviously reached "the point of no return."

At the turn of the century, the threat of world pollution and the idea that mankind would someday be accused of killing its own planet and civilization would have been considered absurd. Now, in 1980, mankind is running scared—and has every reason to do so!

It is apparent that mankind will need more than five smooth stones and a slingshot to face the giant industrial conglomerates that are forcing us to live in a totally hostile environment where even the air that we breathe can kill. We are confronted with an entirely new challenge—survival—in a world of expanding technology that is rapidly altering our surroundings and exposing us to increased amounts of harmful chemical substances, some of which did not even exist a decade ago.

This has resulted in what is called "environmental disease." The danger of this disease to the lives of Americans is staggering, for approximately a thousand new chemicals are produced each year. More than 12,000 compounds are already on the government's toxic-substance list; 1,500 are suspected of causing tumors; 30 compounds currently utilized in industry are known to cause cancer. Many products that support the nation's standard of living, from high-energy transformers to decaffeinated coffee to plastic seat covers, have been made from substances on the list. A pervasive industrial chemical called PCB floats invisibly through air and water. It is brought to the dinner table in fish and other foods, and it is even present in mother's milk. The substance has also been found to cause cancer in laboratory animals.

The twentieth-century technology that has generated today's affluence in America has also created pestilence as deadly as the epidemics of the past, though slower acting. "All we've done is exchange bubonic plague for cancer,"[35] says William Lijinski of the Frederick Cancer Research Center in Frederick, Maryland.

The implications are frightening. The National Institute for Occupational Safety and Health has estimated that 100,000 deaths from on-the-job pollution occur annually, with 390,000 new cases being reported every year. The United States currently has one of the world's highest incidences of cancer associated with pollution—so high that some leading experts conclude that it may be responsible for up to 90 percent of all cancers found. Umberto Saffiotti of the National Cancer Institute says, "Cancer in the last quarter of the twentieth century can be considered a social disease, a disease whose causation and control are rooted in the technology and economy of our society."[36]

But our "purposeful" destruction of America is twofold. Not only are our shortsightedness and blissful ignorance causing an increasing number of deaths, but we are also paving the way for the fulfillment of the apostle John's prediction. We are damaging America's ecology at an unprecedented rate, and in so doing we are "destroying the earth."

Jack Shepherd, former senior editor of *Look* magazine, described the present situation in America quite realistically when he wrote in 1970,

> We are fouling our streams, lakes, marshes. The sea is next. We are burying ourselves under seven million scrapped cars, 20 million tons of waste paper, 48 billion discarded cans and 28 billion bottles and jars a year. A million tons of garbage pile up each day. The air we breathe circles the earth 40 times a year, and America contributes 140 million tons of pollutants.[37]

It appears that we have lost all control. Not only are we guilty of polluting the water and air supply on which we thrive, but now we're also exterminating many kinds of plant and animal life faster than they can reproduce. Plankton, the basic food substance of the sea, now blooms a full month later than it did in 1950, motivating one expert to comment, "These changes could have huge and perhaps catastrophic effects on the ecology of the sea if they continue."[38] The possibility that atmospheric contamination caused by our industrial pollutants will diminish the solar energy that reaches the earth from the sun and create another "ice age" is getting stronger and stronger; some animal species, once plentiful, are now on the verge of extinction. According to the Smithsonian Institution, the extermination of mammals has increased by fifty-five times during the past 150 years, and all remaining species of mammals will disappear within the next thirty years if the killing is not stopped.

A pessimistic view? Not when we consider all the available evidence that vies for our attention via audio and visual media.

In the past few years, a new danger has threatened our environment—a danger some prefer to ignore, for it is insidious; it is one that kills just as indiscriminately as air pollution but has been unrecognized until recently. Known as "acid rain," it is linked to fossil fuel combustion and kills fish and wilderness lake systems and much more. It does not exact human sacrifice of the magnitude that London experienced in 1952 when its deadly smog killed four thousand people in a terrifying four-day invasion, but to a leading American authority on acid rain, Gene E. Likens of Cornell University, it is a threat to the natural life systems.

> One has to be very seriously concerned about this kind of environmental insult on the natural system. . . . There is a limit to the stress they can withstand. The forests and the land are the support systems. Without those life support systems to cleanse the air and the water, to provide food for us to eat, our health is just as much in jeopardy as if something is affecting us directly.[39]

Acid rain can fall anywhere downwind of urban or industrial pollution. The danger is mounting. It now appears to be so widespread that the typical rainfall in the eastern United States and southeastern Canada is about twenty-five times more acidic than it would have been had the rain contained acid from natural sources. According to Lars N. Overein, director of a comprehensive Norwegian study on acid rain, the majority of inland waters have completely lost their fish population as a result of this new pollutant. In the Adirondack Mountains of New York, all fish have disappeared from more than one hundred lakes and streams, but the situation in Canada is most acute. Speaking of the devastating effects of acid rain in that area, author James Gannon worries,

> Around Sudbury, the acid lakes look pure because they are so clear, but that is an illusion. They are clear because for all practical purposes they are dead! The organic life has been virtually erased—fish, amphibians, invertebrates—all gone. Plankton gone. Algae, bacteria, severely reduced or chemically altered. The entire aquatic ecosystem snuffed out—perhaps irrevocably. . . . When the chain of life is broken like this, the higher animals are also affected. Fish-eating birds and vertebrates have left the

lakes. . . . Parts of the barren landscape around Sudbury will
resemble what the earth will be like when life is gone entirely.[40]

Is this what the future holds for us? Will our generation be the one
that will "destroy the earth"? Will our unique "sin," when added
to our other destructive tendencies, be enough to tip the scales of
doom for America and hasten her final and ultimate demise?

The factors that give scientists concern for the future are the
very ones the Bible provides as evidence that God is going to
intervene and save mankind from itself. The message in Revelation 11:18 had no specific relevance in the tide of human affairs
until the overwhelming surge of technological development that
followed on the heels of World War II. Only since the end of
that war has humanity developed the capability to literally destroy the earth.

Christian scholars often refer to Genesis 1:26, which states
that God has given mankind dominion over the earth. The Old
Testament scholar, Walter Brueggemann, interprets this to
mean that humanity has been given the responsibility for
maintenance, order, and control of that which was created on
earth and to safeguard it.

"To subdue and have dominion," Brueggemann says, "is not a
charter for abuse, but rather a command to order, maintain,
protect, and care for."

Can it be that America's violation of this very basic principle
is leading her to her own destruction?

It is a question that undoubtedly demands an answer, but with
its preoccupation with the breakdown of social, economic, and
ethical values, America is beginning to find new ways to cope
with its mounting frustrations. The country had a glorious and
courageous birth and grew into adulthood with the aid of ingenuity and the profits of war. The years following World War II,
however, spawned a multitude of problems that have scarred the
old traditions, and many now look toward a "new beginning" for
America.

A short time before his death in 1975, Arnold Toynbee made a comment about the coming years that seemed almost mythical. "In the 21st century, human life is going to be a unity again in all its aspects," he mused.[41] Did he have a forewarning that the day would come when we have utilized all our available options and that something else, something drastically different, would be necessary to offer humanity one more chance? We will never know, yet in selected laboratories and think tanks in the United States, plans are being formulated to revamp the American dream into the dynamics of the future. At present more than four hundred colleges are offering courses in futurism, and the World Future Society claims approximately twenty thousand members and holds international conferences to ponder new times. The ambiguities of the future have intrigued humanity ever since Joseph interpreted Pharaoh's dream and forecast seven years of plenty and seven years of hunger; and now America appears to be foremost in reaching out for the magic of the future. Is it perhaps because we have lost our faith in the present? H.G. Wells commented,

> All this world is heavy with the promise of greater things, and a day will come, one day in the unending succession of days, when beings, who are now latent in our thoughts and hidden in our loins, shall stand upon this earth as one stands upon a footstool and shall laugh and reach out their hands amidst the stars.[42]

Were his words prophetic or merely expressing the desperate hope of a man lost among the bewildering anxieties of the present?

According to many, our future will be utterly fantastic—so fantastic that it will make us forget all our problems. They're predicting mile-high multipurpose dwellings; space voyages to the outer planets for high school students; a three-day work week; mind-reading computers that will enable a subject to be programmed through electronic impulses and enable an operator to make a machine perform through thought alone; and finally an end to pollution, the menace of the seventies.

Can it be that America is beginning to lose the grasp of reality it once possessed and is starting to grope for a promise—any promise? Perhaps Thomas Jefferson spoke for *our* generation when he voiced his dream, saying, "I like the dreams of the future better than the history of the past."

Has America reached the outer limits?

Chapter Nine

The Missing Soul of the Nation

Perhaps nothing has become so misleading a cliché as that supposedly constitutional phrase "separation of church and state," for in this glib phrase is contained much of contemporary America's greatest spiritual dilemma: How can a nation "under God" permit—in the name of religious liberty—virtual exclusion of everything religious from political, social, economic, and moral life? America's ties to divine authority are a matter of historical record, emphasized by the Founding Fathers, yet a reading of modern Supreme Court decisions indicates clearly that God is now officially being banned from involvement in the life of Americans. The most obvious is the issue involving schools and religion.

Consider the following popular and simple prayer:

> Almighty God, we acknowledge our dependence upon Thee, and we beg Thy blessings upon us, our parents, our teachers and country.

Controversial? Hardly! Not for a Christian anyway, and it is certainly not the type of prayer that is likely to offend the spiritually sensitive. Yet this very prayer, composed by the State of New York and recited in the New York public schools, was deemed unconstitutional in the famous Supreme Court "prayer case" of *Engel* v. *Vitale*. Justice Hugo Black, arguing for the majority, stated that

> . . . the constitutional prohibition against laws respecting an establishment of religion must at least mean in this country it is no part of the business of government to compose official prayers for any group of the American people to recite as part of a religious program carried on by government.[1]

Consider the fact that a culture originating in Christian values and rooted in a nation "under God" has managed to convince itself in a kind of satanical legal twist that reading the Bible in school is "unconstitutional." Yet that is precisely what the *Abington* v. *Schempp* case claimed despite the fact that the Bible has been read in schools throughout American history. In this case Supreme Court Justice Tom Clark in the majority opinion stated bluntly, "In the relationship between man and religion, the State is firmly committed to a position of neutrality."[2]

Of course, the claim that the refusal to allow Bible reading in schools is an example of "neutrality" strains the imagination. True, the courts have permitted the Bible to be read in schools as literature or history, but this permission is an unwarranted condescension—for strict "neutrality" in religion is in fact impossible. The fact that the courts have refused to permit the Bible to be taught in public schools as a religious document and guide means in reality that they have taken an official stand *against* biblical Christianity.

It is a confusing issue, for in other decisions the Supreme Court has upheld the right of the American government to be "neutral" but at the same time "accommodating" to religion. For instance, in the oft-quoted *Zorach* decision, the court ruled that for the states to adjust public events to accommodate Christian holidays was both unconstitutional and "accommodating" to religion. In this same case, Justice William O. Douglas argued that ". . . we find no constitutional requirement which makes it necessary for government to be hostile to religion and to throw its weight against efforts to widen the effective scope of religious influence."[3] Hence, from this strange "accommodation-neutrality" perspective, the court apparently argued that while the government cannot be explicitly Christian in orientation and policy, it can be accommodating to Christianity in a neutral fashion!

Truly a strange and inexplicable ambivalence.

There is little doubt—indeed, it is accepted without discussion—that the Founding Fathers of America were explicitly religious in orientation and their religion was, at least for many, firmly rooted in biblical Christianity. America to them was to be one nation under God, and laws were to be fashioned after biblical principles.

Although some of the Founding Fathers were more deistic than others, the existence of God Himself was not to be doubted. Furthermore, while it is true that the religious motivations of the Founding Fathers and revolutionary leaders of the emerging nation, and especially America of 1776, were diverse and often contradictory, it is clear that *by the time of the Constitutional Convention in Philadelphia in 1787, the Christian view dominated.* C. Gregg Singer states,

> Of greater significance is the fact that very few of the radicals of 1776 found their way to the Philadelphia meeting. Franklin was there, to be sure, but a subdued Franklin in contrast to the philosopher of 1776. Conspicuous for their absence were the most forceful of the liberal deist leaders: Jefferson, Richard Henry Lee, and Thomas Paine. There is abundant evidence that evangelical

Christianity was held in much higher respect by the majority in the Convention of 1787 than it had been in 1776. The Christian world and life view was accorded greater weight by the delegates than . . . in . . . 1776 . . . they were willing to accept the benefits of the Gospel in the political and social life of the American people. . . . The Convention of 1787 displayed a consciousness of the meaning of the doctrine of sin. . . . it is conceded that a . . . Christian philosophy permeated the thinking and action of the members.[4]

Clearly the Constitution itself and its associated Bill of Rights base the guarantees of personal liberty in God, the Creator—the absolute standard. From the landing of the Pilgrims at Plymouth, Americans were recognized to be "endowed by their Creator with certain unalienable Rights" that all were to be viewed as *self-evident*. Rights not urged or arguable, but rather rights obvious to people of all faiths. Thomas Jefferson noted that any effort to build a nation on a footing other than God's will had the historical fact of failure of past efforts with which to contend. He said,

> Can the liberties of a nation be sure when we remove their only firm basis, a conviction in the minds of the people, that these liberties are the gift of God? That they are not to be violated but with His wrath? Indeed, I tremble for my country, when I reflect that God is just; that His justice cannot sleep forever, that a revolution of the wheel of fortune, a change in situation, is among possible events; that it may become probable by supernatural influence!
>
> The Almighty has no attribute which can take side with us in that event.[5]

How then are we to react in a time when religion itself has become so problematical in a nation founded upon God that the schools are afraid to appear religious even in the sense of saying a prayer—even a prayer as harmless as the following one that Whitehead in *The Separation Illusion* notes was judged to be illegal in one of the Eastern states:

> We thank you for the flowers so sweet,
> We thank you for the food we eat,
> We thank you for the birds that sing,
> We thank you [God] for everything.[6]

In Whitehead's provocative and worthwhile book, we are consistently reminded that the concept of separation of church and state has been grossly exaggerated and misconstrued by modern court decisions. In fact, it is Whitehead's premise that the Founding Fathers never intended for the states to be anything other than religious.

The book reminds us that the concept of a secular nation, a nation ruled by political expediency, was unheard of in 1776. To be anti-Christian in early America, he states, was considered a treasonable offense! In Whitehead's words, "Since the basic foundation of the government was Christian, it had to be protected legally."[7] Indeed, Christianity was both the foundation and the framework on which the Constitution and the Bill of Rights were to be interpreted. The entire concept of checks and balances was biblically inspired to curb the sinfulness of mankind. Likewise, it is no coincidence that the separation of governmental powers into executive, judicial, and legislative branches parallels the basic Christian Trinitarian theme—the governing power of the universe resting within a Godhead consisting of Father, Son, and Holy Spirit. Just as the Reformation had dethroned a fallible pope in favor of an infallible document (the Holy Bible), so did the American Revolution dethrone an "infallible" king in favor of elevating the *law* to king. Thomas Paine is quoted as saying, "In America the law is King."[8]

However, even though law was to become king in America, it was never conceived to be what it now has become—a labyrinth of complex rules and loopholes to be manipulated and contorted to fit petty personal and political desires.

So what was law intended to be in America?

Whitehead points to the answer in precise terms. "Law," according to him, is the secular expression of God's will for America. Founded upon a belief in the God of the Holy Scriptures, America was to be *the* chosen nation, implementing for the second time in history the will of God on earth. Government was to be curbed—its only function to assure with minimal interference the collective interaction among the states. As for the states themselves, they were to be Christian in conception and implementation. In fact, it was never doubted that the states would elect Christians of high moral caliber to rule in behalf of the citizenry. This basic Puritan notion was never intended to be "democratic" in the common sense of the word.

Today, every child quickly learns that America is a "democracy" in which all persons theoretically have equal rights and opportunity. Yet the Founding Fathers had a healthy suspicion and distrust of democracy. Commented John Adams, the second president of the United States in 1815,

> Democracy has never been and never can be so desirable as aristocracy or monarchy, but while it lasts it is more bloody than either. Remember, democracy never lasts long. It soon wastes, exhausts, and murders itself. There never was a democracy that did not commit suicide.[9]

What Adams noted is what Christians attuned to biblical prophecy have always known. God's government is never so naive as to be simply and purely democratic. Such "democracies" cannot distinguish among and between persons but rather lump all together as identical. Man was not created equal, but was equally created—and this accounts for the various individual differences that make a democracy hard to govern. God, on the other hand, distinguishes among and between persons. "Law" is divinely given and entrusted by God to particular people to enforce upon all others. Whitehead writes,

> It must be remembered that the term *democratic* appears neither in the Declaration of Independence nor in the Constitution. Actually, when the Constitution is analyzed in its original form, the document is found to be a serious attempt to establish a government mixed with democratic, aristocratic, and monarchical elements—a government of checks and balances. Basically, the Constitution erected a Republic, but ever since its inception the American Republic has been exposed to democratizing influences.
> The Founding Fathers, as the educated elite of their era, re-

jected democracy outright. Their contempt was intensified when totalitarian repression became the dominating feature of the French Revolution. Many of the framers, including George Washington, would have subscribed to John Adams' sharp remark that democracy was "the most ignoble, unjust, and detestable form of government."[10]

America was not to be a democracy. The Constitution, as the supreme law of the land, was to be grounded in God's law for mankind. Rulers were to be elected by qualified persons to enforce these laws and create new ones as needed in harmony with God's ever-unfolding expression. In all cases, the law as politically dictated was to be under the broad and absolute laws of God as revealed in Scripture. Only those sensitive to His wisdom would rule. It was never imagined that everyone, regardless of qualifications, would vote, and it was certainly not envisioned that everyone would be eligible to hold public office. Indeed, long discussions regarding the right to vote for property owners only, to cite one example, were designed precisely to ensure that knowledgeable and devout persons would select appropriate officials. Likewise it was simply taken for granted that political rulers in a nation founded on God's principles would be Christians. So fundamental was this assumption that the absence of any specifically Christian reference in the Constitution is to be attributed to the idea that the federal government had no right to interfere with individual states that were thoroughly Christian-oriented.

Noting the character of the American Constitution leads to one other important fact previously alluded to: America was conceived as a republic, not a democracy. The difference is basic to an understanding of America's plight today. Inasmuch as God chooses and selects both persons and nations to fulfill His ends, His rule over mankind has never been "democratic," and any nation claiming to be under God's special guidance cannot be a real democracy.

Democracies rule by claiming all must adhere to laws, but the laws are recognized as merely products of mankind and capable of being changed at any time by a majority rule. Hence, what is "illegal" today becomes "legal" tomorrow simply by a change in the expressed will of the people. Such a procedure subordinates the will of God to the whims of man. Only if one can claim that a people's collective will is God's will can democracy claim to be Christian; yet, this claim is patently false.

Scripture reminds us repeatedly that God's will is expressed in absolute laws that stand above collective whims. Human beings, as fallen creatures, cannot presume to elevate their collective desires to universal law. God's absolute laws stand forever to remind and curtail fallen creatures. To presume that a "democratic" nation can rule itself in a manner totally congruent with God's intent is the height of self-deceit. David says in Psalm 33:10: "The LORD foils the plans of the nations; he thwarts the purposes of the peoples."

A harsh judgment indeed.

But what is God's plan for governance? How can we recognize a nation that claims to be under God's special care and an instrument of His will?

The answer, Whitehead reminds us, lies in the Founding Fathers' concept of America: This country was to be a constitutional republic—*not* a democracy. America was to be a nation of laws, but not merely laws conceived and created by people. America's laws were to be inspired by God's example in Scripture and curtailed by His intent. The governed would be ruled by Christian leaders using *Christian principles.* Furthermore, only a qualified electorate would vote, with criteria for voting reflecting Christian sensibilities. Thus America would be ruled by a core of essentially unchanging principles. Any other interpretation of the Constitution certainly seems contradictory to the Founding Fathers' intent. Whitehead has appropriately quoted Rushdoony as stating,

> To read the constitution as a charter for a secular state is to misread history, and to misread it radically. The constitution was designed to perpetuate a Christian order.[11]

Since the Founding Fathers saw America as a basically Christian nation, why have Supreme Court rulings gradually eroded this concept until today, in America, religion of any form, especially Christianity, is paradoxically kept separate from all aspects of political life? Whitehead reminds us that the First Amendment to the Constitution states simply that "Congress shall make no law respecting an establishment of religion, or prohibiting the free exercise thereof."

Wrenched from its context and divorced from its historical and political matrix, this amendment has been distorted to mean apparently that the Founding Fathers did not want "politics and religion" to mix. Nothing could be further from the truth. The interpretation of this amendment, as given in Thomas Jefferson's own words, shows that what was intended by this phrase was to build a "wall" to separate church and state. But nowhere in the Constitution is the phrase "wall of separation between church and state" to be found. In fact, nowhere in the First Amendment do the words *church* and *state* even appear. The famous phrase "a wall of separation between church and state" was written by Jefferson to a group of Baptists in 1802—long after the amendment was adopted in 1791. Jefferson did not author the First Amendment or any of the other nine in the Bill of Rights.

Whitehead's masterful analysis points out that the Founding Fathers were primarily worried about excessive federal governmental powers usurping states' rights. With respect to religion, the issue was quite clear: "Religious freedom" was interpreted to mean that the fundamental Christian orientation of individual states could not be endangered by the support or establishment of a federal religion that could override the *state's right to be Christian.*

In 1791, the year the First Amendment was ratified, more than one-third of the colonies already had established churches—Christian churches. Thus the states' primary concern was protecting their basic right to Christian worship and expression, one of the very reasons the Pilgrims left both England and

Leiden. The word *Congress* in the First Amendment clearly meant the federal government; therefore, any "wall of separation between church and state" was to be a wall preventing the federal government from interfering with what was essentially individual state Christianity.

That Supreme Court decisions in future generations would "reinterpret" this amendment to mean a wall must be set up between individual states and their Christian principles is to distort completely the intent of the Founding Fathers. Much of the weight of subsequent Supreme Court decisions rests on Jefferson's private interpretation of this amendment expressed in his letter to the Baptist group, in which his own liberal religious views are interpreted as if they represented the conservative, Christian views of the majority who ratified the First Amendment.

The irony is apparent: the First Amendment, whose true purpose was to protect state Christianity, has become the major obstacle to its realization. Thus, while we have a government of men and laws, it is only of the laws of men, uninformed and unsupported by divine law. Long ago Martin Luther warned of the consequences of this situation when he stated, "Where there are no people who have been made wise through the Word and the Laws, bears, lions, goats and dogs hold public office and head the economy."[12]

The political course followed by successive American congresses has deviated sharply from the future as charted by our Founding Fathers. America has been alienated from God by her own misinterpretations of the principles laid down by her founders. To continue in this direction is to become what can only be considered "un-American"; a nation outside and adrift from God's will; a nation steeped in the arrogance of democracy, rooted in a humanism that, like the Greeks of the past, sees their gods only as inflated men. If America is indeed a nation supported by laws made by man's free will, then what are we to do with the Christian principles upon which the country was formed? Are we to abandon the path so surely illuminated for us by men who recognized the limitations of man? Benjamin Franklin worried, "If men are so wicked as we now see them *with* religion, what would they be without it?"[13]

If there is one single term that captures the essence of these times—that of a nation moving steadily toward total abandonment of religious guiding principles—it is the word *secularization.* Even though the social scientists who use the word continually debate its precise meaning and determinants, they do agree that secularization encompasses the gradual and interminable erosion of religious principles in the practical, everyday life of the people.

The paradox in the process of secularization is that under the very guise of religious freedom, religion as a truly guiding force is diminished. Citizens are encouraged to embrace whatever religion they wish as long as the exercise of their beliefs does not interfere with the prevailing educational, moral, and political decisions of the day. In these "real life" matters, according to the secularists, more pragmatic and purely nonreligious criteria are applied. This means that the actual running of the nation and myriad social institutions is left to persons who either are avowedly *nonreligious* or whose religious beliefs will not influence their daily tasks. The result is a nation either totally and arrogantly irreligious or comprising schizoid individuals, affirming a religious belief they cannot practice effectively in everyday life.

The gradual misinterpretation of the "separation illusion" has meant that, according to Supreme Court rulings, religion *must* be excluded from the public schools. As a pacifier to our troubled minds, the court kindly granted permission to teach a brand of "comparative religion" instead, i.e., a critical look from the "outside" of what various religious faiths believe. But to try to present Christianity as truth revealed by God is regarded as "unconstitutional." Even the most simple prayers are now outlawed. Because of this, the school systems supported by taxes in a nation founded with Christian intent cannot even present these basic truths to young children.

A liberal argument can be made, of course, that such *exclusion* of a particular religion from the school system assures "religious freedom" in a broader context, in that no *single* religion can usurp any other in the classroom. The public schools are then "safe" as a forum for education beyond the influence of any particular religious system. "Freedom of religion" is thus maintained for persons of certain religious persuasions who are able to preach their messages in their own churches or in private schools, where the costs are extraordinary.

To Christian children in modern America, this "religious freedom" is indeed a paradox. They are "taught" knowledge and "reality" in school outside the context of any revealed scriptural truths. Of course, their faith can be affirmed apart from the school system, but the result is inevitably a schizoid child, unable to integrate and practice his religious beliefs effectively. The strangely fragmented world in which the child is made to live under the guise of "religious freedom" is in fact a forced freedom from practicing and living an integrated Christian life. And this is precisely what the Founding Fathers argued against. America was to be the land of religious freedom with the right to practice and live an integrated Christian life. To deny this fully integrative Christian world view is literally to foster a religious tyranny under the deceptive mantle of religious freedom. This secularization of American life is invariably the result of the secularization of the state, which itself is but an end product of a government abandoning Christian principles.

The tyranny of this newfound "freedom" is perhaps best noted in the context of the word *tyrant,* derived from the Greek *tyrannos,* literally meaning "one who rules others outside the sanction of religious authority." Hence, the emergence of a purely secularly ruled America is in fact the emergence of tyranny—not religious tyranny as practiced under the Inquisition, but exactly the opposite —secular tyranny. Whitehead commented, "Undeniably, Christianity is being disestablished in the United States, thereby making way for the establishment of the 'religion' of humanity."[14]

The full terror of this secular tyranny is yet to be revealed, but the lessons of history are suggestive. Nations have toppled for far less important reasons. Yet even more tragic than the existence of a fragmented world in which religion and the state operate separately and remain at odds with one another, the error of secularization ensures that future generations will themselves be fragmented persons, unable to integrate their religion and their everyday, practical life. Dividing culture into the religious and the secular also means dividing the child's mind and creating an alienated being, unable to be healed in a culture that itself is sick. The obvious outcome is a society of estranged and alienated persons who only perpetuate the cycle from which they cannot escape. . . .

The ultimate result of a religion of secularized man will be the proliferation of characteristics now already emerging and known to social scientists as *criteria of alienation*—also identifiable as the inevitable fruits of the secular religion of humanism.

The first criterion is *meaninglessness*, the belief that nothing really makes sense.

Paradoxically this drifting into "meaninglessness" does not originate from a lack of meaning per se, but rather from the very fact that by now so many diverse "religions" and "philosophies" exist, making an intelligent choice difficult. This meaninglessness is encouraged and fostered in public education in which the child is literally forced to learn isolated, abstracted, and fragmented theories of life and is not guided into adopting or adhering to a specific system. For the Christian child, the education to which he or she is exposed is literally a shattering of a previously accepted view of the world. And this is exactly what the Founding Fathers hoped to avoid. A nation whose education is based upon Christian principles can confront other systems of belief from a bastion of firm truth and safety. To take this much-needed anchor away from the child under the illusion of separation of church and state is to virtually cast him adrift in a sea of meaninglessness from which there is no escape.

The second criterion of alienation is an outgrowth of meaninglessness that is all too evident today. Given no single system of meaning to interpret and to guide our conduct, a kind of *normlessness* emerges in which precisely nothing is possible, because "everything is possible."

This caricature of freedom is just another illusion. Whatever we do can be validated if we simply select a philosophy or religion to justify it. Separated and fragmented in belief, people tend to become separated and fragmented in their actions. The validity of the family structure falls to the ax of relativity, and the decline of any absolute system of truth is in itself the new absolute. Everyone acts, no one feels committed, and violations against God's will fail to produce even a sense of guilt. Man has begun to believe the greatest lie: the one that he *himself* is like God, and because of that anything can be legitimized. Yet the very multiplicity of legitimations brings its own dizziness and despair, and a firm awareness of God's reality merges into a fog where, like cats in the dark, all beliefs become gray.

Whitehead terms this new secular humanism the "Eden Syndrome" and states, "Modern man, taken as a whole, has fallen prey to the same temptation Eve fell for in the garden. That is, she desired to be as God, possessing the capacity to determine for herself what is good and what is evil."[15]

God, however, has imposed His absolute standards upon the universe, thus limiting man's capacity to decide certain issues. In light of the "Eden Syndrome," school systems based upon an illusory kind of "separation of church and state" can do nothing but teach the "Eden Syndrome" as the foundation of the new secular reality of our times.

As a final criterion of alienation, the fact of *personal* and *interpersonal* isolation inevitably follows. People are estranged, believing and acting in diverse manners and not sharing common bonds of faith and morality. Individuals clutch at one another desperately, grasping for a strong and lasting love, only to find the bonds irreparably broken almost as soon as they are formed.

Absolute ethics are abandoned in favor of "situation ethics" dictated by changing situations.

It was Nietzsche who warned that when God is finally "dead," all is possible, and in His place he joyously foretold the coming of a new "Superman." Instead, mankind dead to a belief in God lies whimpering and afraid, wrapped in despair as in a cold, damp towel. . . .

There is no doubt that these criteria of alienation—meaninglessness, normlessness, and isolation—describe modern, fragmented man, who masquerades as his own god within a religion of his own making.

The solution?

Benjamin Franklin had an answer when, on June 28, 1778, during a period of great trouble and dissension at the Constitutional Convention, he made this forceful suggestion:

> We have not hitherto once thought of humbly applying to the Father of Lights to illuminate our understanding. In the beginning of the contest with Great Britain, when we were sensible to danger, we had daily prayers in this room for divine protection.
>
> Our prayers, sir, were heard, and they were graciously answered. . . . Do we imagine that we no longer need His assistance? I have lived, sir, a long time, and the longer I live, the more convincing proofs I see of this truth—that God governs the affairs of men.
>
> And if a sparrow cannot fall to the ground without His notice, is it probable that an empire can rise without His aid? We have been assured, sir, in the sacred writings that except the Lord build the house, they labor in vain that build it. . . . I firmly believe this! . . .[16]

Chapter Ten

Where Does America Go From Here?

Where does America go from here? In a letter to the editors of *Time* magazine, U.S. Sen. George McGovern of South Dakota proposed a solution in the "spirit of '76." His comments are both thought provoking and hopeful.

Two hundred years have passed since the American Revolution, and the message of that Revolution has been heard throughout the world. The principles of national independence, representative democracy, and civil liberties which were the basis of our Revolution have served as incentives to countless revolutionaries in Latin America, Africa, Asia and Europe.

Sometimes, however, I think that we have done a better job of exporting our principles than applying them to public policy. Two hundred years after the Boston Tea Party, multinational corporations and monopolistic practices continue to stifle competition and free enterprise. Nearly 200 years after the adoption of the Bill of Rights, the right to dissent is still threatened by governmental action. And, perhaps most ironically, after 200 years we often find ourselves identified with repressive and reactionary regimes abroad.

As the nation approaches the third century of the Revolution, *it is time to reconsider the principles which created the revolution*–and to apply them to the making of public policy [italics ours].[1]

Written a year *before* the Bicentennial, Senator McGovern's words may have stirred a few sporadic comments among *Time*'s readers, but as a whole, the country has become quite callous to admonishment and reproof. Yet his call for a return to "our principles" should not go unheeded, for America is built on a set of principles that are unprecedented in the world's history and there is little doubt that much of the success of the United States lies in the Constitution's acceptance of the biblical view of the nature of man.

There is, however, a puzzling aspect to the role and destiny of America in this latter part of the twentieth century. George Washington's vision on the Valley Forge battle area during the winter of 1777, as related in chapter 1, clearly pointed toward the grim events of the Revolutionary War and the Civil War; but it went a step further. The vision also directed Washington's attention toward another dramatic encounter between outside forces and those of the United States. While the vision has been given to us in such a way as to suggest a near-devastating military conflict to be fought out on U.S. soil, prophetic interpretation will allow it also to be taken spiritually as well—i.e., a major conflict between the forces of Good and Evil.

Washington quietly watched history unfold in the misty depths of his vision, according to Anthony Sherman, and then commented,

"'Then once more I beheld the villages, towns and cities

springing up where I had seen them before, while the bright angel, planting the azure standard he had brought in the midst of them, cried with a loud voice, "While the stars remain, and the heavens send down dew upon the earth, so long shall the Union last." And taking from his brow the crown on which blazoned the word "Union," he placed it upon the standard while the people kneeling down said, "Amen."

"'The scene instantly began to fade and dissolve, and I at last saw nothing but the rising, curling vapor I at first beheld. This also disappeared, and I found myself once more gazing upon the mysterious visitor, who, in the same voice I had heard before, said,

"'"Son of the Republic, what you have seen is thus interpreted. Three great perils will come upon the Republic. The most fearful for her is the third. But the whole world united shall not prevail against her. *Let every child of the Republic learn to live for his God,* his land and Union [italics ours]."'"

The vision definitely emphasizes responsibility to God *before* country. Is this what is happening in this land today? Are we really putting God first?

Many Americans live with a constant feeling of impending doom—as if the pendulum of destiny has ticked off the required number of hours and time is finally beginning to run out, leaving us to the whims and uncertain mercy of the unknown.

Some are attempting to take steps to prevent what has been called the "inevitable" and look for solutions to America's ills on the political level, mindful of the dominant feeling in the Soviet Union that world forces are moving inexorably in their favor. They—the Russians—believe that the era of American predominance in world affairs—in fact, the American civilization *itself*—is ending, and that Soviet supremacy is already a reality.

Whether this is a correct interpretation of the multitude of unresolved issues facing the United States is a subjective judgment. U.S. Sen. Howard Baker of Tennessee is one statesman who does not share this view, although he admits it exists. He says,

There is a growing feeling that the United States has no rational, coherent foreign policy, at least not one that asserts the role of greatness and strength that the United States has always, or at least since World War II, exhibited to the world. Some have said in Europe . . . that it is no longer safe to follow the lead of the United States because the United States no longer has the will to lead. I don't believe that. I think a few things can be done that would clearly signal that the United States still relishes the role; at least welcomes the role of guardian and protector of those who wish to be protected in the free world.[2]

But can this be done while we are lacking in moral fiber? Is there a political solution to the dilemma created by the combination of moral indifference, political opportunism, social disintegration, and the inevitable results of our mad, mad race toward unrestrained hedonism?

Friedrich A. Hayeck, economist at the University of Salzburg in Austria and an astute impartial observer of the American scene, blames the dilemma on democracy. He says,

I am alarmed at the speed at which democracy is losing its reputation throughout the western world. Yet in my view it would be wrong to say that democracy has failed and therefore is *doomed.* We must distinguish between democracy as such and the specific institutions Western nations have been using to realize democracy. *It is the failure of these institutions that tends to discredit democracy today.*

Democracy as we know it today, is suffering from a mistaken construction of its institutions. It combines legislature and government in the same body. Government thus becomes "unlimited" by law. The legislatures we have today, in other words, are mainly governmental bodies. Their powers are not limited by any law they cannot alter. Many believe democracy must mean "unlimited government." But "unlimited government" is inherently weak [italics ours].[3]

Rene Dubois, professor emeritus at the Rockefeller Institute, adds,

Democracy is going through one of the most fundamental steps of its evolution in modern times. . . . We are having to improve our participatory democracy through people themselves than through laws. . . . I think that people have made the wrong demands on democracy.[4]

Whatever the demands, "the people" indeed exhibit an increasingly negative mood of apathy and skepticism toward their system of government. This is evident, for example, in the fact that in the 1978 off-year elections fewer than 36.1 percent of all voting-age Americans went to the polls. One votor commented, "It really doesn't make any difference whether you vote or not. They do what they want to anyway—and even then it doesn't work out."

Moral traditions, ideals of hard work, self-restraint, and sacrifice too are eroding in the widening expression of "me-ism" that has resulted in rising delinquency, declining standards of education, family disintegration, and a breaking away from traditional religious values. The nation that once believed in *e pluribus unum* is now highly fragmented by race, sex, ethnicity, and geography, straining a fragile democratic consensus and raising persistent questions about democracy's chances of survival.

Is it really democracy's fault, and if it is, can something be done to reverse the trend and save our institutions?

In Washington in February 1979, author James Michener made some statements that caused some influential heads to bow in thoughtful consideration. Worried about the illness of the national spirit, he cautioned,

> There seem to be great tides which operate in the history of civilization, and nations are prudent if they can estimate the force of those tides, their genesis, and the extent to which they can be utilized. *A nation which guesses wrong on all its estimates is apt to be in serious trouble if not on the brink of decline* [italics ours].[5]

Michener was being extremely kind, expressing conservatively the thought that we are in trouble. Realism speaks harsher language and uses a different vocabulary when describing our present condition. By now we are all clamoring for a workable solution to America's ills—but where is the prescription that will heal?

Lately voices have been raised proposing a Constitutional Convention, an event that certainly would be unique, for none has been called since the gavel called an end to the Constitutional Convention of 1787. The proponents of such a move believe this may well be the vehicle that will provide the answers to many of America's ills. Never before has there been such strong sentiment to convene one. But as promising as it may seem to some legislators, the fear of what might happen if all factions of this divided nation take part in the process keeps many others from endorsing it. The politicians who inhabit the halls of Congress have a growing uneasiness about such a move and fear that they will be venturing into a legislative no man's land where radicals will have a heyday. Yet there is no denying that the Founding Fathers made provisions for such a convention if and when the demand is sufficiently great; Article V of the Constitution provides that a convention *will* be called when at least two-thirds of the state legislatures petition Congress for one. There is no confusion on the subject. Alexander Hamilton made this perfectly clear in Federalist Paper No. 85: "The words of the article are peremptory. Congress *shall* call a convention. Nothing in this particular is left to the discretion of that body."

An overriding fear among opponents is that a convention could become pandemonium, a free-for-all that will not solve anything but hand the country a totally new form of government, created by radicals and liberals, infiltrated with clauses to guarantee affirmative action, outlawing abortion, guaranteeing gay rights, banning school busing for integration, severely curtailing the power of the judiciary, and enacting such articles as to transform our present form of government into a "benevolent" dictatorship where everything is preprogrammed and nothing of any consequence is left to the legislature. Howard Jarvis, the inventor of California's Proposition 13 on taxation, says, "A convention would give every crackpot a chance to write the supreme law of the land."[6]

Still others feel that the very threat of a Constitutional Convention will be sufficient to force Congress to legislate far-reaching changes that will finally enable the country to rise to the challenge and rebuild America, using the old time-proven principles. Realists to the core, framers of the Constitution knew that there might be times when even the best of governments would resist the will of the people it claims to serve; so even without being used, Article V can exert that type of pressure and force the government to initiate the changes needed to turn the tide.

Nevertheless, the real solution does not lie in "new innovations," new Constitutions, new laws, or even a stricter adherence to the laws that have quietly been inserted in the lawbooks of the nation. The real solution lies in a return to the old values. In our modern culture, these ultimate values are still available and are to be found in the Word of God. Our task is not so much to look to the future for new solutions, but to look to the past to values that have been abandoned. Technological solutions—and there is even a "technique" for the formulations of new laws and a new Constitution—are never the answer to violations of a spiritual nature, and only the culture that remains committed to ultimate spiritual values has any chance of survival. Martin E. Marty, Professor of History of Modern Christianity at the University of Chicago, says,

> To find a new program, to build national community, and to develop some common moral language is not guaranteed to produce good people. Such activities will not eliminate evil, bring about personal moral regeneration, save souls, gladden sad hearts or bring in the kingdom of God, utopia or even certainty.[7]

A change in the political life of America is certainly not the answer that will turn the tide. Perhaps we should look for counsel to 2 Chronicles 7:14, where we find the absolute guideline for total transformation. God says to King Solomon,

"If my people, who are called by my name, will humble themselves and pray and seek my face and turn from their wicked ways, then will I hear from heaven and will forgive their sin and will heal their land."

We have literally gone beyond the point where we can effect a change in America without the help of God. America is sick today because we have a spiritual malady; we have forgotten our maker.

At the height of one of our greatest national tragedies, the Civil War, in 1863, President Abraham Lincoln recognized the desperate need for God in national affairs, and he prayerfully issued this proclamation:

> We have been the recipient of the choicest bounties of heaven. We have been preserved, these many years, in peace and prosperity. We have grown in numbers, wealth, and power as no other nation has ever grown; *but we have forgotten God.* . . . We have forgotten the gracious hand which preserved us in peace, and multiplied and enriched and strengthened us; and we have vainly imagined, in the deceitfulness of our hearts, that all these blessings were produced by some superior wisdom and virtue of our own. Intoxicated with unbroken success, we have become too self-sufficient to feel the necessity of redeeming and preserving grace, too proud to pray to the God that made us;
>
> It behooves us, then, to humble ourselves before the offended Power, to confess our national sins, and to pray for clemency and forgiveness;
>
> Now therefore, in compliance with the request, and fully concurring in the views of the Senate, I do by this my proclamation designate and set apart Thursday the 30th day of April, 1863, as a day of national humiliation, fasting and prayer. . . . All this being done in sincerity and truth, let us then rest humbly in the hope authorized by the divine teachings, that the united cry of the nation will be heard on high, and answered with blessings no less than the pardon of our national sins, and the restoration of our now divided and suffering country to its former happy condition of unity and peace."

Lincoln did not look for a solution *away* from God; he begged for a solution for our national maladies *in partnership with God.* This feeling of national dependence on godly guidance is part of our national heritage.

U.S. Sen. Jesse Helms of North Carolina pointed this out in simple and straightforward language when, during the Bicentennial, he counseled,

> God has given us ample means and abundant grace to use in our work of restoring the role of His law in our demoralized country. . . . Each of us has a part to play in bringing about the greatest spiritual awakening that must come upon this nation before we are brought to our knees by the just chastisements of God. Each of us, then, must place our hope and reliance in God, and in that hope and reliance turn our energies to restoring a government and society that serves us as sons of God.
>
> We must turn to the Author of Liberty to enjoy again what once we had so abundantly.[8]

Where does America go from here?

All the curves are leading to national catastrophe unless there are some noticeable changes in our approach to solving our problems. For us, there no longer is a remedy apart from God. There is no healing, no reconstruction, and no renewal of our lost values as long as the principles upon which this country was founded have been relegated to a dusty place in the corners of history.

Reapply godly principles—and live. . . .

Continue to reject divine guidance—and decay. . . .

Our ancestors recognized these basic truths in which great civilizations are rooted.

Can we do less?

Notes

Chapter One

[1]Ellen G. White, *The Great Controversy* (Mountain View, Calif.: Pacific Press Publ. Assoc., 1950), p. 290.

[2]Arturo Gonzalez and Gloria Gonzalez, "The Old Comers Come Home," in *Holiday* (Nov.-Dec. 1976): 34, 66, 79.

[3]Sir William Brereton, *Travels*, as quoted in Kate Coffey, *The Mayflower* (New York: Stein & Day, 1974), p. 35.

[4]Gonzalez and Gonzalez, "The Old Comers Come Home," p. 34.

[5]White, *The Great Controversy*, pp. 290-91.

[6]William Bradford, *History of Plymouth Plantation* (New York: Barnes & Noble, 1959, repr. of 1908 ed.), p. 46.

[7]Ibid., p. 44.

[8]Gonzalez and Gonzalez, "The Old Comers Come Home," p. 79.

[9]Henry Martyn, vol. 5, p. 70, as quoted in White, *The Great Controversy*, pp. 291-92.

[10]*History of the Puritans*, vol. 1, p. 269, as quoted in White, *The Great Controversy*, p. 292.

[11]Martyn, vol. 5, pp. 70-71, as quoted in White, *The Great Controversy*, p. 292.

[12]Bradford, *History of Plymouth Plantation*, p. 79.

[13]Albert B. Osborn, *Finding the Worth While in Europe* (New York: Robert McBride & Co., 1923), p. 59.

[14]*Stars and Stripes* (December 21, 1950).

[15]Charles Colson, *Born Again* (New York: Bantam Books, 1977).

[16]Thomas Paine, *The Rights of Man*, in *The Writings of Thomas Paine*, vol. 2, 1779-1792, ed. M. D. Conway (New York: AMS Press, 1967), pp. 258-518.

[17]Ibid., Editor's Introduction, p. 262.

[18]Robert Bellah, "Civil Religion in America," in *American Civil Religion*, ed. R. E. Richey and D. G. Jones (New York: Harper Forum Books, 1974), pp. 21-44.

[19]Ibid., p. 23.

[20]Ibid., p. 25.

Chapter Two

[1]Phillip Rieff, *The Mind of the Moralist* (New York: Viking Press, 1959).

[2]Otto Friedrich, *Going Crazy* (New York: Simon and Schuster, 1975).

[3]H. J. Eysenck, "Effects of Psychotherapy," in *Handbook of Abnormal Psychology*, ed. H. J. Eysenck (Los Angeles: Knapp Press, 1960).

[4]Karl Menninger, *Whatever Became of Sin?* (New York: Hawthorn Books, 1973).

[5]Leo Srole et al., *Mental Health in the Metropolis: The Midtown Manhattan Study*, 2 vols. (New York: McGraw-Hill, 1962, 1963).

[6]David L. Rosenhan, "On Being Insane in Insane Places," in *Science* 179 (1973): 250-58.

[7]Quoted in *Time* (April 12, 1976):24.

[8]H. M. Ruitenbeck, *Freud and America* (New York: Macmillan, 1966).

[9]J. Herbert Fill, *The Mental Breakdown of a Nation* (New York: Franklin Watts, 1974).

[10]David Riesman, *The Lonely Crowd* (New York: Doubleday, 1953).

[11]James Q. Wilson, "Crime and Punishment," Bicentennial Essay in *Time* (April 26, 1976):82-84.

[12]Ibid.

[13]Anton T. Boisen, *The Exploration of the Inner World: A Study of Mental Disorder and Religious Experience* (New York: Harper & Row, 1971, repr. of 1936 ed.).

[14]Paul Blumberg, "An Authority Tells Why Status Symbols Keep Changing," in *U.S. News & World Report* (February 1977):42.

[15]Ibid.

[16]Rene Noorbergen, *Secrets of the Lost Races* (Indianapolis: Bobbs-Merrill, 1977).

[17]Arnold J. Toynbee, *A Study of History*, 2 vols., abridg., ed. D. C. Somervell (New York: Dell Publishing, 1965).

[18]Ibid., vol. 2, p. 394.

[19]Ibid., pp. 394-96.

[20]Alexandr Solzhenitsyn, "As Breathing and Consciousness Returns," in *From Under the Rubble* (Boston: Little, Brown, 1975), p. 22.

Chapter Three

[1]E. A. Wallis Budge, *The Book of the Dead: Papyrus of Ani* (New York: G. P. Putnam's Sons), pp. 5-6.

[2]Johannes Riem, *Die Sintflut in Sage und Wissenschaft* (Hamburg: Agentur des Rauhen Hauses, 1925), p. 7.

[3]Hugh Miller, *The Testimony of the Rocks* (New York: John B. Alden, 1892), p. 284.

[4]John A. Wilson, *The Culture of Ancient Egypt* (Chicago: Univ. of Chicago Press, 1956), pp. 41-42.

[5]George Rawlinson, *A History of Ancient Egypt* (New York: Nottingham Society), p. 146.

[6]Arthur Weigall, *The Life and Times of Akhnaton*, (London: Thornton, Butterworth, 1922), pp. 127-28.

[7]Wilson, *The Culture of Ancient Egypt*, pp. 41-42.

Chapter Four

[1]Uriah Smith, *The Prophecies of Daniel and the Revelation* (Nashville: Southern Pub. Assn., 1944), p. 16.

²James Wellard, *Babylon* (New York: Schocken Books, 1974), pp. 156-57.
³H. W. F. Saggs, *The Greatness That Was Babylon* (New York: New American Library, 1962), p. 307.
⁴*Encyclopaedia Britannica* (Chicago: William Benton Publisher, 1968), 11:41-42.
⁵James G. MacQueen, *Babylon* (New York: Frederick A. Praeger, 1964), p. 151.
⁶Smith, *Prophecies of Daniel and Revelation,* p. 45.
⁷Herodotus, trans. A. D. Godley, books 1 and 2 (London: William Heinemann, 1966 ed.), pp. 190-91.
⁸Smith, *Prophecies of Daniel and Revelation,* p. 48.

Chapter Five

Two excellent source books for the information in this chapter are—
C. M. Bowra, *The Greek Experience* (New York: World, 1957).
M. I. Finley, *The Ancient Greeks* (New York: Viking, 1963).

Chapter Six

¹Kenneth D. Matthews, *The Early Romans* (New York: McGraw-Hill, 1973).
²Ugo Enrico Paoli, *Rome—Its People, Life and Customs* (New York: David McKay, 1963).
³Philip Van Ness Myers, *Rome: Its Rise and Fall* (Philadelphia: Richard West, repr. 1901 ed.), pp. 10-11.
⁴Will Durant, *Caesar and Christ,* The Story of Civilization, vol. 3 (New York: Simon and Schuster, 1944), p. 391.
⁵John P. Balsdon, editor, *Roman Civilization* (Baltimore: Penguin Books, 1969), p. 182.
⁶A. H. Jones, *The Later Roman Empire* (Oxford: B. Blackwell, 1964), p. 1063.
⁷E. B. Castle, *Ancient Education and Today* (Baltimore: Penguin Books, 1961), p. 120.
⁸Jerome Carcopino, *Daily Life in Ancient Rome* (New Haven: Yale Univ. Press, 1960), pp. 120-22.
⁹*The Modern Romans* (Pasadena, Calif.: Ambassador College Press, 1975), p. 29.
¹⁰M. L. Clarke, in J. P. Balsdon, *Roman Civilization,* p. 208.
¹¹Castle, *Ancient Education and Today,* p. 124.
¹²Carcopino, *Daily Life in Ancient Rome,* pp. 106-7.
¹³Mikhail Ivanovich Rostovtzeff, *Rome,* ed. J. Elias Bickerman, trans. J. D. Duff (New York: Oxford Univ. Press, 1960), pp. 322-23.
¹⁴William Stearns Davis, *The Influence of Wealth in Imperial Rome* (New York: Macmillan, 1913), pp. 314, 335.

Chapter Seven

¹Our historical overview is adapted from Toynbee's classic study of history. See

Arnold J. Toynbee, *A Study of History*, 2 vols., abridg., ed. D.C. Somervell (New York: Dell Publishing, 1965).

[2]Herbert J. Fill, *The Mental Breakdown of a Nation* (New York: Franklin Watts, 1974).

Chapter Eight

[1]*These Times* (October 1978):26.

[2]*U.S. News & World Report* (March 8, 1976):50.

[3]Ibid., p. 51.

[4]Ibid., p. 55.

[5]*U.S News & World Report* (November 27, 1978):56.

[6]Gene H. Hogberg and Jeff Calkins, "Does America Still Stand for Anything?" in *Plain Truth*, vol. 11, no. 21 (January 1976).

[7]Ibid.

[8]"Tomorrow: The Republic of Technology" in *Time* (January 17, 1977):36.

[9]Ibid., p. 37.

[10]*U.S.A. Today* (October 1978).

[11]"The Family" in *Time* (April 12, 1976).

[12]"Life in America" in *U.S.A. Today* (December 1978).

[13]*The Modern Romans* (Pasadena, Calif.: Ambassador College Press, 1975), pp. 21-22.

[14]*National Enquirer* (March 25, 1975).

[15]Ibid.

[16]"Religion" in *U.S.A. Today* (September 1978):20.

[17]Quoted by John R. Price, *America at the Crossroads* (Indianapolis: Christian House Publ. Co., 1976), pp. 244-45.

[18]Ibid.

[19]*National Enquirer* (February 4, 1975).

[20]Richard Wheeler, *Pagans in the Pulpit* (New Rochelle, N.Y.: Arlington House, 1974), p. 89.

[21]Harold K. Schilling, "The Role of the Church in Higher Education," paper presented to the American Baptist Education Assn. at Drake University, Des Moines, 1958.

[22]Rene Noorbergen, *Jeane Dixon—My Life and Prophecies* (New York: William Morrow, 1969), p. 153.

[23]*Time* (November 21, 1977).

[24]"Sixty Minutes," CBS Television Network (March 6, 1979).

[25]*Plain Truth* (Nov.-Dec. 1977):17.

[26]"Behavior" in *Time* (April 5, 1976).

[27]*Time* (January 8, 1979):48.

[28]*Time* (June 30, 1975):14.

[29]*U.S. News & World Report* (November 27, 1978):25.

[30]Ibid.

[31]*Time* (June 30, 1975):18.

[32]Ibid., p. 17.